To: Jeff Fleischer...
Thank you for always being
there and for years & years of
memories!! :) Wishing you a
lifetime of happiness! You
deserve nothing less!
All the Best!! :)

Kathryn Tropp

THE KICKIN' HOOSIERS

THE KICKIN'

HOOSIERS

Jerry Yeagley and Championship Soccer at Indiana

Kathryn L. Knapp

QUARRY BOOKS

AN IMPRINT OF
INDIANA UNIVERSITY PRESS
BLOOMINGTON AND INDIANAPOLIS

This book is a publication of

Quarry Books

an imprint of
Indiana University Press
601 North Morton Street
Bloomington, IN 47404-3797 USA
http://iupress.indiana.edu

Telephone orders   800-842-6796
Fax orders   812-855-7931
Orders by e-mail   iuporder@indiana.edu

The paper used in this publication meets the minimum requirements of
American National Standard for Information Sciences—Permanence
of Paper for Printed Library Materials, ANSI Z39.48-1984.

Manufactured in the United States of America

Library of Congress Cataloging-in-Publication Data
Knapp, Kathryn L., date
 The kickin' Hoosiers : Jerry Yeagley and championship
soccer at Indiana / Kathryn L. Knapp.
      p.   cm.
 Includes index.
 ISBN 0-253-21741-5 (pbk. : alk. paper)
 1. Indiana University, Bloomington—Soccer—History.
 2. Indiana Hoosiers (Soccer team)—History.
 3. Soccer—History. I. Title.
 GV943.7.I43K63 2004
 796.334'62'09772255—dc22
                                2004009432

1 2 3 4 5 09 08 07 06 05 04

Facing page: Despite the cold and snow, fans flocked to Columbus, Ohio, to cheer the Hoosiers to victory in the 2003 NCAA Championships. Photo: Paul Riley, IU Athletics.

Next page: IU goes through an easy workout the Saturday before the 1999 NCAA Championship game. The Hoosiers defeated UCLA 2-1 in the semifinal match, in quadruple sudden-death overtime, then moved on to face Santa Clara in the final. Photo: Chris Howell, *The Herald-Times.*

CONTENTS

FOREWORD

It's hard to describe my forty-one years at Indiana University. I spent the majority of my life as a coach at IU and watched the soccer program grow from a club team to one of the top programs in the nation. I nurtured it and truly believed in each and every one of my players. We all had a mission to make Indiana University the best soccer program in the country.

Kathryn L. Knapp has done an exceptional job of looking back at all forty-one years. The book itself talks about the individual seasons, the championships, the heartbreak, and most of all the IU soccer family. Over forty-one years, we created a family atmosphere that can't be replaced. It's unique and ever-growing. This book is full of memories from the soccer family. It's well written and easy to read. It tells the story of a struggling club team and its fight to be the best. The IU team started as the ugly duckling of the soccer community and eventually became a swan. The story behind IU men's soccer is that if you believe, anything is possible.

Enjoy!!
Coach Jerry Yeagley
IU Soccer Head Coach 1963–2003

THE INDIANA UNIVERSITY SOCCER PLAYER
The Heart of the Indiana University Soccer "Tradition of Excellence"

Inspired through Personal Motivation

The IU Soccer Player responds positively to external motivation. However, his strength and inspiration is derived primarily through personal motivation. The IU Soccer Player has a burning desire to achieve success and is driven to be the best he can be.

Performance Follows Attitude

The IU Soccer Player's performance is shaped through a positive attitude. While the performance of others is inhibited by anxiety and a fear of failure, the IU Soccer Player's performance is bolstered through courage and confidence. The IU Soccer Player demonstrates positive self-worth, always striving to build up his teammates.

Integrity

The IU Soccer Player is an honest player. He strives to do everything right all of the time. He takes no shortcuts and does not cheat in practice or in games. While others save it for just the game, the IU Soccer Player challenges himself to get better every day. He holds himself and his teammates accountable to the highest standards.

Pride in the Uniform

The IU Soccer Player takes tremendous pride in wearing the soccer uniform. He has a deep respect for the history and tradition of the program and for those who have previously worn the uniform. The IU Soccer Player considers it an honor and a privilege to wear the uniform; and he recognizes the responsibility that goes with this honor. Only the highest standard of performance and best effort is acceptable. When the IU Soccer Player takes the field wearing the IU colors, he holds his head high, never hoping to win, but rather always expecting to win. After all, he is the Indiana University Soccer Player.

A NOTE FROM THE AUTHOR

Before I even attended college, I heard the buzz of Indiana soccer. People said that it was the best program in the nation. I was friends with guys on my high school soccer team who raved about going to camp and being in Bloomington. But it wasn't until I attended IU that I caught the IU soccer bug. It didn't take long. I attended my first adidas Classic in 1994 and haven't missed one since. There was something special in the air. The fans were excited to be there, and the players always gave it their all. Then I met Coach Jerry Yeagley. He was a class act from the first moment we met. His players were no different. They've all been an inspiration to me.

It's refreshing to know that there is one sport at IU that won't let fans down. When life gets rough and things get out of control, there is one thing you can always rely on—IU soccer. The team will always put on a good show. They will always compete. They will always play with heart. And they will almost always win.

I decided to write this book for one simple reason: IU soccer deserves coverage. It tends to get overshadowed by other sports on campus, but it may be the one sport whose players truly compete for the love of the game. It's about having a true passion for the game of soccer.

I want to thank the IU soccer family, especially Jerry and Marilyn, for their support and for believing in me. This book wouldn't have been possible if it weren't for their cooperation. I'd also like to thank my mom for being my second pair of eyes; Kathleen Marie for allowing me to live at her place; my dad for helping me develop a passion for sports; my friends and family for all their support; the IU Athletic Department, the *Arbutus*, the IU Archives, and other photographers for providing great images; Gary Fresen for providing me with the club statistics; and the IU Media Relations Department for providing me with the team statistics and the lists of All-Americans and letterwinners. And lastly, I'd like to thank Indiana University Press for giving me this opportunity. I hope you all enjoy reading the book. I know I've thoroughly enjoyed putting everything together.

Thanks for the memories!!
Kathryn L. Knapp

Jerry Yeagley celebrates his
500th win during the 2001 season.
He ended his thirty-one-year
varsity career at IU with 544 wins,
the most by any collegiate coach.
Photo: Paul Riley, IU Athletics.

THE KICKIN' HOOSIERS

1

A Storybook Ending

Every story deserves a perfect ending, and every coach should go out on top. But in real life, these things don't often happen—unless you're Jerry Yeagley. Yeagley arrived at Indiana University in 1963. He would spend the next forty-one years coaching the IU men's soccer program. He turned a club sport into a varsity sport, and then into a soccer powerhouse. Prior to his thirty-first season as varsity coach, Yeagley announced that 2003 would be his last. Little did he know that he was in for the ride of a lifetime.

The season started with a win and ended with a celebration. December 14, 2003, was a day that will live in the hearts of the Indiana University soccer family forever. It marked a storybook ending for the only coach the men's soccer program had ever known. Red and blue confetti littered the sky as snow fell to the ground. Cheers arose from all around Crew Stadium in Columbus, Ohio. The IU Crabb Band belted out the IU Fight Song, as fans attempted to run out onto the field. Amid all the chaos, the Hoosiers lifted their

The Hoosiers hoist Coach Jerry Yeagley onto their shoulders after winning their sixth NCAA Championship. After the worst start in team history, the 2003 season had a storybook ending for a legendary coach. Photo: Kathryn Griffin, 2004 *Arbutus.*

coach above their heads in celebration. Jerry Yeagley had done it. He had led his team to win the national championship, the sixth for the club. Better yet, he had wrapped up his coaching career as the winningest coach in Division I history.

2003, Here We Come

In Yeagley's final season as head coach for the Hoosiers, a lot was on the line. Could Yeagley become the all-time winningest coach? Could the Hoosiers win another national championship? Once the playing began, the focus shifted to what really mattered—getting the ball into the net and winning a game. IU began the season 2-3-4, the worst start in team history. Everything seemed to be against the Hoosiers.

With a win against Michigan on October 5, IU's performance took a turn for the better. The Hoosiers did not lose another game, ending the season 17-3-5, and winning their tenth Big Ten and sixth NCAA Championship. Yeagley summed up the season with a smile: "I couldn't have scripted it better myself."

The Worst Start Ever

The Hoosiers started the season on a positive note, winning the adidas/IU Credit Union Classic for the first time since 1998. They posted a 3-0 victory over the University of California, and it appeared that scoring was not going to be an issue. The next night, however, the dark cloud that would hang over the program for the next nine games began to form. IU and the University of Alabama at Birmingham battled to a 0-0 tie. The score gave IU the Classic title, but it showed that the scoring might not come all that easily. IU outshot UAB 17-11, with two shots on goal, but the Hoosiers failed to finish any attempts.

Next up for IU was a rough five-game road trip. The Hoosiers headed east to the

University of Connecticut Classic, where they added a loss and a tie. They lost to the Fighting Irish at Notre Dame before finding some luck against Fresno State. IU tallied three goals again and won the match 3-1. Perhaps three was their lucky number. "I think the team was focused," junior forward and co-captain Ned Grabavoy said. "But when you're losing, it's hard to be positive. It was almost like we were waiting for something bad to happen. Once we got on the right track, we gained confidence."

The team returned to Bloomington to kick off the Big Ten season against Michigan State on September 21. The Hoosiers fell victim to the black cloud again, ending the night in a 1-1 draw. Five days later, IU hosted Penn State. The Hoosiers looked tough, dominating the game with a 2-0 lead against the No. 15 Nittany Lions. But then the black cloud started pouring down rain. Lightning forced the teams to head to the locker rooms for what was expected to be a slight delay with just 23:31 remaining in the second half. Two hours later, the referee called the game. Unfortunately for the Hoosiers, the game was just three and a half minutes shy of complete. It would have to be rescheduled for November.

"We knew we had to win the game against Penn State," midfielder Pat Yates said. "They were ranked pretty high. We knew that if we beat them it would look good. We were up 2-0, just killing them. And our luck—it started raining and lightning, and there was nothing they could do. It was terrible. When the referee said the game would be canceled, Penn State's locker room went crazy."

The Hoosiers had a six-day break before facing in-state nemesis Butler. It was a game they had all looked forward to, but at the end of the match, IU walked off the field with another 1-1 draw. "We expect to win every game, but this was a game we were real confident about," said Hoosier midfielder Brian Plotkin. "We said before that game, this will be the game that will change our confidence. After that game, the locker room was really quiet. The coaches didn't know what to say. That was probably the lowest point of the season."

Yeagley did have one thing to say. He gave the team a one-sentence speech that would linger in their minds for days to come. "After that Butler game, Coach Yeagley came in, and he had a blank stare on his face," Yates remembered. "He looked at all of us. He didn't say anything for like two minutes. The only thing he said was, 'Maybe I should have retired last year.' And he walked out. I remember him slamming the door to the coach's office. Everybody just looked at each other." Midfielder and co-captain Danny O'Rourke was haunted by that speech. "Those words were ringing in my ears for days," he said.

After nine games, the Hoosiers' record sat at 2-3-4—the worst start in IU history. It was time for the coaches and players to reevaluate their situation. It

Danny O'Rourke challenges a Michigan State player for possession of the ball in IU's first Big Ten game of the season on September 21. The match ended in a 1-1 tie. Photo: Paul Riley, IU Athletics.

no longer mattered whether Yeagley would break the all-time record. The Hoosiers had to regain their confidence and find a way to make things happen. "You know, we're 2-3-4," Yeagley said with a smirk. "The only thing left for us is to be number one."

Those words seemed to spark a change in the Hoosiers. They traveled up to Michigan for their second Big Ten match of the year. The game got off to a stressful start for Indiana as Michigan's Matt Niemeyer tallied a goal at the 18:05 mark. IU struggled to gain control of the match, firing ball after ball at the net, but failing to finish. The Wolverines sped up and down the field, fighting to maintain control. But IU refused to give up. The crowd in Ann Arbor was sprinkled with cream and crimson, and the Hoosier fans were cheering loudly for their team. In the second half, the game would become IU's. Just three minutes into the half, Michigan's Kevin Savitskie took down a Hoosier in the box. The referee awarded IU a penalty kick. Ned Grabavoy stepped up to the line to take the shot. He buried the ball into the net, evening the score at one apiece.

The Hoosiers began to push even harder, blasting shot after shot toward the net. But, so typical of the rest of the season, nothing went IU's way, and the game went into overtime. It was the Hoosiers' seventh overtime of the season, and they had yet to win one of those matches, with a 0-2-4 record. It was left to speedy freshman forward Jacob Peterson to give the team the extra boost it needed. Just two minutes into the overtime period, Grabavoy sent a ball to an open Peterson on the left side of the field. Peterson flicked the ball past Wolverine goalkeeper Peter Dzubay and directly into the net. It took eight overtimes, but the Hoosiers had finally won an overtime match.

"We went up to Michigan after a good week of practice," O'Rourke said. "We fi-

nally got our confidence back. I think that Michigan game we had a big huge rock on the top of a hill, and we just couldn't get it over that hill. Winning in overtime gave us confidence."

No one knew it at the time, but the game would mark a new beginning for the Hoosiers. "At the beginning of the year, the first nine or ten games, I didn't even feel like I was an Indiana soccer player," goalkeeper Jay Nolly said. "I felt like I was messing their tradition up. There are so many people that follow our team that are not physically around us. It felt like we were letting everybody down. It was to the point where we just hit a wall. And we said, 'This is our team. This is our experience. We need to turn it up and play.'"

The Winning Continues

After the Michigan game, the Hoosiers continued their road trip, dominating two Big Ten teams. They shut out Wisconsin 3-0, then stopped in Evanston, Illinois, on their way back to Bloomington. Again they dominated 3-0, en route to a winning record of 5-3-4. "Against Michigan I thought, great, another overtime game," Nolly said. "And then we won it. We took a ton of confidence into playing. We went to Wisconsin and Northwestern and we shut them both out. We had total confidence for the young guys."

IU then returned to Bloomington. Could the team extend their streak on their own field? The Hoosiers were normally unbeatable at Armstrong Stadium, but at this point in the season they were 1-0-3 at home. It didn't take long for the squad to prove that they were for real. They quickly added three more wins to their record, defeating IUPUI, Ohio State, and St. Louis. The St. Louis game (October 24) marked the first time anyone had scored on the Hoosiers since their visit to Michigan nineteen days earlier. In that five-game stretch, IU scored twelve goals and allowed just one. Not too shabby for a team that had started off on such shaky legs.

"We felt like we were playing well," Plotkin said. "Just little things weren't going our way. We put a lot of emphasis on the little things and finding a way to win. Where in the beginning we weren't looking for a way to win, we were finding a way to tie. Once we became responsible for ourselves, the whole team became responsible for each other. We got the ball rolling with a couple of victories and just kept it going."

The Hoosiers ended the month of October with a 2-0 victory at Louisville. They then welcomed Kentucky on November 2. The two teams had faced off in the preseason, with Kentucky handing Indiana a 2-1 loss. That game hadn't counted against IU's record, but now, everything mattered. Hoosier senior midfielder Vijay Dias wasted no time getting the Hoosiers on the board. Plotkin passed to Dias, who sent the ball into the net at the 9:27 mark. Kentucky spent the rest of the game attempting to equalize, but to no avail. IU held on for the 1-0 victory—the Hoosiers' tenth win of the season.

The next weekend, the Hoosiers would play their final regular-season game of the year. The match marked a special event: it was Yeagley's last regular-season game, and it was a make-up game for IU and Penn State. The Nittany Lions took the field with a vengeance. They tallied two goals in the first half and took a 2-0 lead into intermission. The Hoosiers, however, had a tendency to win games in the second half—and that's just what they did. Sixteen minutes into the half (61:31), Grabavoy took control of the ball and sent it to a running Pat Yates. He sent the ball into the net, putting the Hoosiers just one goal behind Penn State. Nine minutes later, defender Drew Moor added a goal. And at the 83:37 mark, Plotkin headed

Ned Grabavoy jumps up for a header vs. Ohio State on October 18. IU won the game 3-0. Grabavoy finished the 2003 season as the team's leading scorer, with eleven goals and eleven assists. Photo: Paul Riley, IU Athletics.

the ball home, giving IU a 3-2 lead. The Hoosiers held on for the 3-2 victory in what may have been the most exciting match of the season.

"This was a thriller," Yeagley said. "I've never been more proud of a team wearing the IU uniform, coming back the way they did. They played together and for each other. It was a total team effort. I will remember this one."

According to Nolly, taking the game up a notch in the second half was what the Hoosiers did best. "We were such a strong first-half team with how we played, but were a second-half team by how we finished," Nolly said. "That was where we won our games. I don't think we ever won a game in the first half. We'd wear the teams down in the first half, and then second half we'd put on the pressure. I've never been with a more fit team than our team."

The Hoosiers ended the regular season on top of the Big Ten. It was a great way for Yeagley to end his regular-season career.

Big Ten Champions

IU hosted the annual Big Ten Championship November 13-16. The Hoosiers sat out the first round with a bye, then faced Wisconsin in the second round. The weather soon became a factor for both teams on a cold, miserable night in Bloomington. It would be seventy-eight minutes before either team could register a goal. But when it came time for someone to break the 0-0 draw, IU's Pat Yates stepped up to the task. "Mr. November" tallied his third goal of the season, giving the Hoosiers a 1-0 lead. That one goal proved to be enough, and IU ended the night with a 1-0 win.

Two days later, IU faced Penn State in the championship match. The Hoosiers had defeated the Nittany Lions just eight days earlier, but that game was history. This was a championship game, and all

that mattered now was the present. This time the Hoosiers tallied first, when Plotkin sent his sixth goal of the season into the net at the 23:56 mark. Before the half ended, Penn State's Mike Lindemann evened the score at one apiece. Neither team got on the board in the second half, and regulation ended with the score still tied 1-1.

Again no one could score during the overtime period, and the game went into penalty kicks. Moor stepped up first for the Hoosiers, easily sending his shot into the lower left corner. Penn State's Gabe Bernstein then took a shot for Penn State. The ball grazed off Nolly's hand and went into the net, tying the penalty kicks at one apiece. Grabavoy kicked next for IU and easily finished. Nolly then stepped up big for the Hoosiers, making his first save of the PK round. IU's Vijay Dias took the Hoosiers' third attempt and sent it into the net. Nolly again made a save against Joe Zewe, giving IU a 3-1 advantage. One more PK, and the Hoosiers would win the championship. Plotkin stepped up to the line, paused for a second, and sent his shot toward goal. It went directly into the lower left corner of the net. The Hoosiers erupted in celebration. They had just won their tenth Big Ten Championship, and in dramatic fashion. "We practiced penalty kicks in training," Yeagley said. "We picked the ten players who would take the shots. They chose their own order and buried them."

After the conference tournament, two Hoosiers had decisions to make. Ned Grabavoy and sophomore defender Drew Moor had received call-ups from the United States Under-20 Team. If they said yes, they would represent the United States in the World Youth Championships but would miss most of the NCAA Tournament. If they said no, they would miss out on a unique opportunity. Both players chose to play at the World Youth

Jed Zayner takes control of the ball during an early season match. Zayner became a stellar part of the Hoosier defense and was named Big Ten Co-Freshman of the Year. Photo: Paul Riley, IU Athletics.

Championships. "It's a chance of a lifetime," Grabavoy said. "How could we turn that down?"

NCAA Tournament, Look Out

After twenty matches, IU's record stood at 12-3-5. The Hoosiers had overcome all obstacles, ending the Big Ten regular season in first place and winning the conference championship. Now the moment had arrived that all the players were waiting for: a run in the NCAA Tournament. At this point, any loss would bring an end to Yeagley's career. But the Hoosiers were

hot. They had not lost a match in thirteen games, since September 18. However, they were missing two starters in Grabavoy and Moor. The NCAA awarded the Hoosiers a No. 8 seed in the tournament standings. They would sit out the action in round one and wait impatiently for round two. "Everyone is so happy, especially after the start we had," Plotkin said. "We want to win as much as we can for Coach. It would be great to put him on top."

IU hosted Kentucky in the second round of the tournament. The two teams had battled it out just three weeks earlier, with IU coming away with the 1-0 victory. But this time they were starting from scratch, and the stakes were much higher: The winning team would continue on, and the losing team would end its season. The Hoosiers hit the field on fire. Their offensive push brought the fans to their feet. In the twenty-third minute of play, midfielder Josh Tudela was taken down from behind, and IU received a penalty kick. Dias stepped up to the line for the Hoosiers. He shot, and Kentucky keeper Andy Gruenebaum grabbed the ball for a save.

Kentucky intensified its attack, scoring the first goal of the match at the 25:49 mark. But before the end of the first half, Peterson, helped by Tudela and Dias, would even the score. In the second half, no one scored, despite ten shots by Indiana and four by Kentucky. The Hoosiers were starting off NCAA play with yet another overtime game—their ninth of the season. Both teams battled to gain control. But just over three minutes into the period, Kentucky's Peter McLellan took down IU's Danny O'Rourke with a tackle from behind and received a red card. Despite Kentucky's one-man deficit, the Hoosiers could not find the net.

In the second overtime period, Yeagley put Greg Badger into the lineup to give the Hoosiers a fresh set of legs. It was a good decision. Five minutes later, Badger scored, giving IU the 2-1 win. "With ten minutes to go in the final overtime period, how can we generate a little more offense?" Yeagley said. "The players asked for Badger. They have a lot of confidence in him. He's a guy who is dangerous in practice around the box and in the penalty area. He puts his body on the line. That was a great goal. It wasn't the prettiest, but it was one of the best." It may not have been pretty, but it was good enough to give the Hoosiers the win.

Next up for IU was Virginia Common-

wealth University. On a cool, windy day in Bloomington, play got off to a slow start. Both teams came out attempting to put on pressure, but they managed to get off only three shots each in the first half. The second half was a different story. Just nine minutes in, VCU's McColm Cephas collected his second yellow of the match. He left the game, and the Hoosiers then took their play to a whole new level. At the 62:09 mark, Plotkin buried a penalty kick into the net, giving IU the 1-0 lead. Nine minutes later, Tudela added a goal. Six minutes later, Peterson sent a six-yard shot into the net. Six minutes after that, Yates sent an unassisted ball into an open net. And as if that weren't enough, Jordan Chirico chipped the ball over the goalkeeper's head at the 89:44 mark. The crowd erupted with joy as the Hoosiers won easily, 5-0. Once again, they had proved to be a second-half team.

"When we're losing and it comes down to halftime, we don't even talk about what we did," defender Jed Zayner said. "The coaches say, 'OK, that's over. You already know what you did wrong. This is a new half. We're gonna win this half and we're gonna win this game.' Coach Yeagley always picked us up and always knew how to do it."

Chirico scored the last goal ever for Yeagley at Armstrong Stadium. The Hoosiers would travel for the remainder of the tournament. The crowd gave the coach a standing ovation as he raised his hat to them in gratitude.

The Hoosiers then boarded a plane and headed out west to play top-seeded UCLA on the Bruins' home field. It would be perhaps the toughest match-up for Indiana in 2003. The Hoosiers now had a chance to prove themselves to the entire country. Rumor had it that UCLA would end Yeagley's career, but the Hoosiers and their fans had other plans. Hundreds of fans came out to support

IU, along with the Crabb Band. The fans celebrated prior to the game at alumni functions. They arrived at Drake Stadium ready to cheer the Hoosiers on to victory.

"Any time you go away, especially out in California, you wonder who is going to be there," O'Rourke said. "We were practicing, and UCLA had their techno music playing. All of a sudden, we see Andre Luciano, one of the big supporters of the program, come out yelling 'Hooooosiers!' Everyone looked at each other like, are you serious? Then we heard the band coming down the walkway playing the IU Fight Song, over the speakers and over everything."

"We took over the UCLA crowd," Nolly added.

It took the Hoosiers a couple of minutes to get into the swing of things. UCLA's Chad Barrett put on the pressure and tal-

lied a goal just over ten minutes into the first half. IU quickly snapped out of it, and John Michael Hayden equalized just over four minutes later. With a 1-1 score, the two teams battled it out until the bitter end. With the clock ticking down, the Hoosiers took possession. Peterson saw a chance and took it. The ball bounced off the post directly to Yates's feet. He took a shot and gave IU a 2-1 advantage.

"Peterson hit an unbelievable ball from five yards outside the 18," Yates said. "I was already making a run because I had my defender beat. I just kept making the run after that shot. It hit the bottom of the crossbar, and the keeper was diving. It hit the crossbar so hard that it hit him. It bounced right in front of me on stride. If I had missed it, that would have been completely my fault."

With just seconds remaining on the

Brian Plotkin celebrates during the team's 5-0 rout of Virginia Commonwealth in NCAA play. Plotkin tallied the first goal of the match, converting a penalty kick. As a sophomore, he became the team's second leading scorer, recording seven goals and nine assists. Photo: Paul Riley, IU Athletics.

clock, the Bruins continued to try and even things out. They took a shot that just barely rolled wide of the side bar. "My heart just stopped," Yates said. "That ball was harder to miss than it was to make. That's for sure. A guy headed it first, and it just dropped right in front. The other player hit it across, and the ball just went straight across the line out of bounds. I thought for sure it was a goal."

With that, the IU fans took a collec-

Pat Yates celebrates after scoring the game-winning goal vs. UCLA in the quarterfinals of the NCAA Tournament. IU won the match 2-1 en route to the College Cup. Yates was nick-named "Mr. November" for his outstanding play in the tourna-ment. Photo: Paul Riley, IU Athletics.

tive breath and started counting down. The tears began to flow and the fans be-gan to celebrate. The Hoosiers had done it—they had upset the No. 1 seed in the tournament en route to the College Cup. "We knew it would be a tough game," Plotkin said. "If we could get in there and play our game, we'd find a way to win. It was scary when they scored ten minutes in and we were down 1-0. We came back and scored less than five minutes later. After Yates scored, it was the scariest ten minutes ever." Yeagley himself stood on the field incredulous. "Can you believe it?"

he uttered to all those who congratulated him. But believe it or not, IU was headed to its sixteenth College Cup.

Six-Time NCAA Champions

IU was no stranger to the College Cup, men's soccer's version of basketball's Fi-nal Four. The Hoosiers had been there fif-teen times in the past. In fact, every four-year player in the Hoosiers' program had played in a College Cup. IU had advanced to the final game eleven times in those fifteen years, taking home five champi-onship titles. One more championship would give Yeagley and his Hoosiers the most won by any university in Division I history.

The Hoosiers were riding an unbeat-en streak of fourteen games. Just two more wins and they would win the na-tional championship. First up was un-seeded Santa Clara. The teams had met a total of five times, with the Broncos edging IU 3-2 on victories. But the Hoo-siers had won their last two meetings in College Cup play, defeating Santa Clara 4-0 in the 1998 semifinals and 1-0 in the 1999 final. The teams would face off in the second match of the evening.

The fans arrived at Crew Stadium in Columbus, Ohio, dressed for the cold. As predicted, the temperature dropped as the wind picked up. The first match-up saw No. 6 St. John's upset No. 2 Maryland by a score of 1-0. Then Indiana and Santa Clara took to the field. Early on, the game turned into a battle in the midfield. Ev-eryone looked to get chances, but none of the offensive attempts were converted into a goal. The scoring lull lasted for ninety minutes of regulation, sending the teams into a blustery overtime period.

Just before the end of the second over-time, in the 104th minute, the Hoosiers finally found the net. Freshman midfielder Josh Tudela sent a pass upfield to Plotkin. He saw an open Yates and flicked the ball in his direction. Yates jumped up and headed the ball into the top left corner of the net, giving IU the 1-0 victory. "I don't think anyone expected this young team to play for the national championship," Yeagley said. "What an accomplishment. These freshmen aren't playing like freshmen anymore."

Win or lose, Sunday, December 14, 2003, would mark the final game of Yeagley's career. The tension mounted as Indiana took the field to face St. John's. Just two days earlier, the Red Storm had upset Maryland. They looked tough, but so did the Hoosiers. As an added bonus, Grabavoy and Moor had returned to play in the championship game. Grabavoy arrived in Columbus on Saturday night, while Moor arrived hours prior to the game. They dressed and took their places in the starting eleven.

Grabavoy wasted no time getting the Hoosiers on the board. Just fifteen minutes into the match, a St. John's defender leveled Peterson. The referee called a freekick. Grabavoy and Plotkin stood on either side of the ball. When it came time to take the shot, Grabavoy completed the task. He bent a perfect ball just inside the right goal post, giving the Hoosiers the 1-0 advantage. "I haven't made a freekick all year," Grabavoy said. "This one gets the monkey off of my back. When I stepped up to take it, I just looked at Plotkin and he knew. Sometimes you just have that feeling before you kick the ball. You know it's going in."

Four minutes later, Peterson himself took charge. He dribbled upfield and sent an unassisted blast into the net, giving the Hoosiers a 2-0 lead. Before the end of the half, St. John's looked to counter, but couldn't finish anything. IU keeper Jay Nolly was busy, forced to make six saves. In the second half, the Red Storm's pressure continued as the snowfall increased. St. John's took nine shots, and Nolly re-

sponded with four more saves. At the 78:03 mark, St. John's Ashley Kozicki finally found the net. "I told the guys at halftime that the team they're beating 2-0 was down two goals and a man in NCAA Tournament play and came back to win 3-2," Yeagley said. "There's no quit in St. John's. There wasn't any quit tonight."

The game turned into a one-goal battle. If the Red Storm scored, they could send the match into overtime or play to win. The Hoosiers barely got off two shots. But now IU was focused on one thing—a defensive battle. The defenders bunkered in around the net and made sure to stop any chances that St. John's took. With time running out, Nolly jumped up and grabbed the last save of the game. IU held on and won 2-1. "Everybody overlooked us," defender Jed Zayner said. "They said, 'Look at this freshman team with four or five freshman starters. That's not usually how the Hoosiers do it.' We changed it up a little bit this year. Coach always likes to be the underdog, overlooked because the heart of the Hoosier always comes out. It's true."

The team jumped with joy in celebration as the IU soccer family wiped away tears. Was it really possible that the Hoosiers, after starting the season 2-3-4, had just won the national championship? It was indeed possible, and Yeagley's career ended on the highest of notes—a national championship celebration. "I've been trying not to think about me," Yeagley said. "This day is about the team. I did have the strangest feeling, though. I asked the guys in the locker room if this was a dream or if this was real. It's hard to explain. I couldn't be any happier for our guys. We've had other teams get a star on their uniform, but I don't think any team has come this far to achieve so much. That's what's special about this championship."

When interviewed on national televi-

Coach Yeagley celebrates with the team after winning his sixth national championship. It was the final game of Yeagley's forty-one-year career—and it may have been the biggest win of them all. Photo: Paul Riley, IU Athletics.

sion, Yeagley was speechless. His players pride themselves on that moment. "That's not like Coach; he always has a word to say," Nolly said. "It's great to make him speechless. Stuff just happens to Coach. He's one of those guys where things just turn out for him."

Yeagley received the 2003 adidas/National Soccer Coaches Association of America (NSCAA) Coach of the Year award and ended his career as the winningest coach ever in Division I history, with a 544-101-45 (.821) record over his thirty-one varsity years at IU. In ten years of club play, he had led his club to winning records in every season. He took home six NCAA Championships and ten Big Ten Championships. He had a truly

stellar career and capped it off with his sixth national Coach of the Year title. Yeagley retired on top after a storybook ending to his final season. It doesn't get much better than that!

"I hope our season helped Coach end on a good note and with good memories," Danny O'Rourke said. "If it weren't for him, I don't think IU soccer would be where it is today. Who knows, there might not even be IU varsity soccer if he hadn't started it. I think everyone has already tipped their hats to Coach. I personally want to thank him for giving me the opportunity to play here and believing in me. By believing in all his players, we were able to win games and national championships for him. He's just a great man and a great ambassador to soccer. He'll be missed. He will not be forgotten, ever. He's the man."

Next Up

With Yeagley stepping down as head coach, the IU Athletic Department announced that Assistant Coach Mike Freitag would take over the program. Freitag will be joined by former Hoosiers Caleb Porter, Todd Yeagley, and Sean Phillips. The quartet will welcome back the national champions after losing only a few players. And if 2003 was any indication of what the heart of the Hoosier consists of, anything is possible in 2004.

The players are ready to return to action, and they don't look negatively at 2004. "Last year we lost a lot of people and weren't really favored to do anything," O'Rourke said. "This year we'll have the monkey on our back coming in. We return basically everyone from last year. Everyone will be gunning for us. We will have to take a different mentality. We'll get pumped to play other teams, but they'll be even more pumped than us. We've got to take our level up another notch. It's going to be an exciting year. Not only that, but we'll have not a new coach but a new head coach. I don't think of Freitag as a new coach because he's been there for so long. I don't think we'll really skip a beat at all. Coach Freitag is of the same mold as Coach Yeagley. We've got the coaching staff to repeat. We've got the players to repeat. And the mentality of this team is strong enough to repeat."

The Hoosiers look to be in top form in 2004. And as they've proved over and over again, they can never be counted out. They're in it to win, and will do whatever it takes to make that happen. That's the Hoosier soccer tradition.

It Starts with the Family

When Jerry Yeagley took over the IU Soccer Club, the first page of a forty-one-year success story was written. He built what was primarily a social club into a powerhouse varsity program. Along the way, he also began to build the IU soccer family. That family includes wife Marilyn, daughter Yvette, son Todd, and the hundreds of thousands of people whose lives he touched along the way. It includes the players, their families, the support staff, club attendees, camp staff, fellow coaches, and devoted fans. The IU soccer family follows the Hoosiers throughout the country and roots them onward to success. There may not be a more loyal family out there.

On February 14, 2004, the size of that family became apparent when almost a thousand people gathered at a retirement celebration for Coach Yeagley. Current players, past players, club players, their families, and friends of the program traveled from across the globe to honor Jerry and Marilyn for their dedication to IU soccer. It was a night full of memories.

Hundreds of former Hoosiers gathered on February 14, 2004, to honor their coach and celebrate his retirement. They also kicked a ball around during the morning hours. Once a soccer player, always a soccer player! Photo: Paul Riley, IU Athletics.

"It's tough to compare soccer coaches to other coaches because a lot of people don't know them," former player Ernie Yarborough said. "When Dean Smith retired from North Carolina, I watched ESPN the next morning. They interviewed all these people. All of them spoke of family, tradition, discipline, character, professionalism, great guy, great coach, class, integrity, and knowledge of the game. Every single thing that they said could have easily been said about Jerry Yeagley. But it wasn't, because A, he wasn't retiring, and B, he coaches soccer, not basketball. So he won't be on *Sports Center*. They won't interview him because he's not coaching a high-profile sport. But that's how important he was to his era, his game, and the university."

The Man behind the Program

Jerry Yeagley was raised in Myerstown, Pennsylvania, a small town in the heart of Pennsylvania Dutch country. He grew up in a small home with his parents, Harold and June, and two sisters, Connie and Janie. Yeagley's parents were both musicians, but they were also very athletic. They encouraged him to be active from an early age. He played trombone and piano and enjoyed spending time at the local playground.

One summer at the playground, the park supervisor, a gentleman by the name of Barney Hoffman, showed Yeagley and his friends the game of soccer. Little did young Jerry know, but soccer would become the ticket to his destiny. Hoffman also taught physical education and coached at Myerstown High School. When it came time for Yeagley to go to high school, he decided to join the sports teams. He played soccer in the fall, basketball in the winter, and baseball in the summer. He chose soccer over football because at that time in Myerstown, there were no options. "We

didn't have other games," Yeagley said. "It was the only sport in the fall. I was a pretty good basketball player. As a matter of fact, I averaged nearly twenty points a game. But we were a small school, and it wasn't high-level basketball, whereas soccer was strong in that part of Pennsylvania. In baseball, I was average. Soccer was my strongest sport."

Yeagley helped lead the way when Myerstown beat Upper Darby High School 2-0 in the state championship in 1958. With fewer than 200 students, it was the smallest school to win the title. "They had about 4,500 students in senior high. We had 160 if that," Hoffman recalled. "There was no classification. There was no real state championship. It was mythical. It was our district playing a Philadelphia district. We beat District One and beat a team that hadn't been scored on in twenty-two games or beaten in twenty-six games."

Yeagley had a knack for shutting down the opposition. In the championship game, he played a big part in handing Upper Darby the shutout. "Jerry took on their top boy, and he more or less destroyed him," Hoffman said. "We had seven fouls in the first half, and six of them were on Yeagley. It wasn't anything deliberate. This was their playmaker. Second half I told him not to worry about it—that we'd win on our own terms. It was 0-0 at the half, and we scored two goals and won."

When it came time to make a decision about college, Yeagley looked to Coach Hoffman for guidance. "He being my early role model and hero, I wanted to be like Barney," Yeagley said. "I wanted to be a teacher and a coach. He encouraged me to go to West Chester, against the wishes of my family somewhat. I had two uncles—one was a doctor and the other a dentist—they wanted me to go into medical fields. My parents would have preferred that, I believe. But I was very much interested in teaching and coaching, and that's the direction I went."

Sitting in the stands at the high school championship game was West Chester men's soccer coach Mel Lorback. He liked what he saw of Yeagley and invited him to attend West Chester. Another member of Yeagley's high school team, Bill Fulk, was also recruited by Lorback. The duo headed to West Chester, and in another four years they won another championship. "We both went to West Chester together," Yeagley said. "We both played on the national championship team together as seniors. That was a unique experience. As seniors we played in a state championship, and as seniors we played in a national championship."

Yeagley played on a championship-caliber team all four years in college. West Chester made it to the semifinals of the NCAA Tournament in each of those years. The NCAA began keeping official records in 1959. In 1961, West Chester defeated two-time champion St. Louis 2-0 to win the championship.

Yeagley played midfielder in high school but switched to defender in college. He had a passion for shutting down top players. "I loved the challenge to shut down an opposing striker [forward]," Yeagley said. "I played with pretty much reckless abandon. I'd put my body on the line, and I was always a fierce competitor. I wasn't the most gifted soccer player. I was good, but I wouldn't consider myself a star." An all-around athlete, he also played on the college tennis team in the spring.

Yeagley's collegiate studies focused on physical education. He still intended to become a physical education teacher and coach like his role model, Barney Hoffman. Yeagley also began to watch his college coach very closely. Lorback had much

success and became Yeagley's second role model. "I learned an awful lot from Mel Lorback," Yeagley said. "He was a military guy. He was very strong and disciplined on organization. Nothing was left to chance. I learned a lot about those aspects from him. From Barney I learned the passion of the game, the love of the game, and I learned how to play. Between the two of them, I fashioned an early philosophy of my own. I took from each of them and inserted my own personality."

After college, Yeagley took a shot at playing "professional" soccer. "In those days they didn't have professional soccer; it was semi-pro and in a loose manner," Yeagley said. "You got twenty-five dollars for playing, and if you won you got fifty dollars. There was a league centered around Philadelphia—the American Soccer League. I played for a club out of Philadelphia." But Yeagley's playing career was short-lived. "In the very first game I played, I broke my leg playing against Reading," he said. "That sort of ended my professional career. It was a pretty complex fracture. I graduated in a walking cast."

Yeagley looked to his mentors for advice. Encouraged by Lorback and other faculty members to go on to graduate school, he enrolled at the University of Pittsburgh and received a Ford Foundation Scholarship. In the mornings he taught at a local junior high school; at night he attended his graduate courses. He received his master's degree in 1963 and began his search for a job.

Yeagley had a number of job opportunities, but he chose to hold out for one that really appealed to him. "In those days, all students had to take physical education courses," Yeagley said. "They needed professors, instructors, who could teach a wide variety of activities. Being pretty well rounded in sports, I had an opportunity

Marilyn Filbrandt raked in beauty queen awards during her collegiate career. Here she was named Arbutus Queen for the 1963–1964 school year. Photo: *Arbutus* Archives, 1964.

for several positions, but I chose to come to Indiana." For Yeagley, perhaps it was a case of knowing the right people. Coincidentally, the dean at Pitt, Dr. Orman, was friends with Dean Daniels of IU's School of Health, Physical Education, and Recreation (HPER). "Dr. Orman took an interest in me and strongly encouraged me to come out to Indiana and interview for the position," Yeagley said. "He highly recommended me. Through his recommendation and hopefully a good interview, I was hired in 1963 to be physical education instructor to teach a variety of activities."

The rest, as they say, is history. Yeagley came to IU, where he would spend the next forty-one years turning the Hoosier soccer program into one of the top men's soccer programs in the nation.

The Woman behind the Man

Sharing the halls of HPER with Yeagley was a young woman by the name of Marilyn Filbrandt. She was active in student activities, cheerleading and pom-poms, Kappa Alpha Theta sorority, and the steering committee of the IU Foundation. Marilyn had grown up in South America, and she noticed that a familiar game was being played in Woodlawn Field across from the Theta house. But she didn't think much of it. Little did she know that her future husband was coaching literally yards away from her.

Marilyn's roommate set her up with a member of the club soccer team, Bob Jones. The two went out, but Marilyn didn't take it too seriously. Jones, however, thought they were dating. He invited Marilyn to accompany his family to Vail over Christmas break, but she couldn't leave campus because she was student teaching. Jones then asked if she could drive him to the airport, and she agreed. He picked Marilyn up in a strange car. When she asked whose car it was, he told her it was Coach Yeagley's, and that she was to park it in the parking lot at HPER after returning to Bloomington. When she got back, she parked it in the HPER lot closest to the Theta house. When Yeagley went out to get his car, he couldn't find it. He looked up the number for the Theta house and gave Marilyn a call.

"Coach called and said, 'Ms. Filbrandt, this is Coach Yeagley, and I'm looking for my car,'" Marilyn recalled. "'You are?' I asked. 'I parked it in the parking lot near HPER.' He said, 'Do you realize there are five parking lots around this building?' So I explained to him where I parked it."

A few days later, the two met face to face. Marilyn and a couple of her sorority sisters were staying in the Theta house over winter break. They had been eating at the Indiana Memorial Union for days. None of them had a car, but they were feeling the need for a change of scenery. When Marilyn was asked whether she knew anyone with a car, Yeagley came to mind. She called and asked if they could borrow his car to go to the new College Mall. He said sure, as long as she had it back by nine o'clock, because he had a date. "I said, 'Good, he's not married. No explanations need to be made,'" Marilyn said. "I just knew that Bob used to rave about this man and what a wonderful person he was. I thought, well, if he's that wonderful, he'll take pity on these Thetas. He came over, and we all piled in. I said, 'He's kind of cute.' I guess we kind of flirted. While at the mall we bought a thank you card. We drove to his apartment, and he drove us back to the Theta house. We gave him his little gift, and then he took us back to the house and he moseyed on. A couple days later he called, and that's how it all started."

After that, they saw each other every day. By the time Bob Jones got back, his soccer coach was dating his "girlfriend." But for Jerry and Marilyn, it was love at first sight. Because Marilyn was a student and Yeagley was teaching in HPER, the dean suggested that they wait a while to take it to the next level. Yeagley proposed in June, after Marilyn graduated, and the two were married in September. Bob Jones stood up in the wedding party. Marilyn became a physical education teacher in Bloomington while she supported her husband's coaching endeavors.

The Family Begins

Although they already had a number of sons on the field, Jerry and Marilyn added two children of their own to their family. Daughter Yvette and son Todd traveled with them on road trips and were raised with soccer at the center of their lives. "We grew up in a unique environment," Yvette said. "The way my parents included us in everything is amazing. It developed in us such a loyalty to the program and what they accomplished. I don't know how they did it. They made us feel every bit as important to them."

Coaching occupied a lot of Yeagley's time, but he did his best to be there for his children's activities. "I remember him going to watch me play hockey, and making the trips here and there," Todd said. "He watched me play Boys Club basketball when I was young. As busy as I know he was, it's amazing that he sacrificed as much as he did to make it as normal a childhood as possible."

Yeagley also found time to teach his children the important things in life. "He'd always try to teach little lessons, whether it was at home or when we were out," Todd said. "He was very big on respect and manners. Growing up, I think those were the things that were instilled in him by his parents. I think he did the same with us. It was very important. He was strict but fair growing up. But he'd put the fear in you."

In everything his children did, Yeagley

Top: Marilyn, Todd, and Yvette stand behind Coach Yeagley as he is honored at his retirement dinner. Photo: Paul Riley, IU Athletics.

At Jerry Yeagley's retirement dinner, he thanks Marilyn for always being his coach. Photo: Paul Riley, IU Athletics.

encouraged them to do their best. He gave them a taste of competition from an early age. "He gave us a very strong desire to win and excel in everything," Yvette said. "He always allowed us to choose whatever made us happy. He was very supportive of dancing and the sports I played. At auditions, it never occurred to me that I wouldn't make it. He also taught us to be graceful in defeat. Be very respectful of those that do well, even if they do so well that they beat you."

Yeagley made sure he kept his family involved in his soccer program. He wanted to share his successes with them. The family went to games together, recruited together, and both celebrated and commiserated together. They were involved in every single aspect of the program. "When we recruited, we did it as a family," Marilyn said. "The players came to our home. Our kids were like younger brothers and sisters to those players. My daughter's first crush was on a player. And Todd, they used to beat up on him and he'd come back for more. It was a family, an extended family. We knew nothing else."

Yvette said that every time they went to recruiting dinners, she was a little nervous. She knew they'd be spending quality time with these players, and after a while she got picky. "We had a huge extended family of big brothers and eventually little brothers," Yvette said. "We had Thanksgiving with them. We vacationed with them. We lived with them for four years. We spent more time with the players than some people do with their own families. It's hard to put into words the way they've touched our lives."

Todd would eventually suit up in the cream and crimson as a member of his father's team. He played at IU from 1991 to 1994, during some of the most successful years of the program. Coach Yeagley described that time as a bonus four years. Todd could not have imagined playing soccer anywhere else. However, he had to prove himself before his father would add him to the team. And once he did, Yeagley blocked all recruiting calls from other coaches. "I made it clear that once he felt I was capable of playing here, this is where I wanted to be," Todd said. "He was very honest. It wasn't until maybe my junior year when he said, 'It looks like you can play here.' He always said if I wasn't good enough, I wouldn't be here. He was always brutally honest with me, and I respected that. That motivated me even more to play here. It would not only be a letdown for myself, but for him and all the alums. They kind of all took ownership of my development too. It motivated me to get better."

As a member of the Hoosier squad, Todd dazzled the alums with his talents. And in 1994, he had the opportunity of a lifetime to win a national championship with his father. Unfortunately, the team fell short in a 1-0 loss to Virginia. It's always hard to lose in a championship game, but that day it was even harder. "The toughest game was when Todd was a senior and the team lost to Virginia," Yvette said. "I didn't know who to feel worse for,

my dad or my brother. And, of course, my mom was blubbering beside me. She's my comrade in arms at these games. That's a little black mark on his career. All four of us wanted desperately to win. That would have been an irreplaceable accomplishment for them to share."

Nine years later, Yeagley and Todd would win a championship together, but this time they were sharing the bench. After playing for Major League Soccer's Columbus Crew for seven seasons, Todd retired and joined his dad on the Indiana coaching staff. They spent Yeagley's last year coaching side by side.

The bond that Jerry and Marilyn share is an inspiration to everyone around them,

Jerry and Todd Yeagley celebrate IU's 4-1 semifinal win over UCLA in the 1994 NCAA Tournament. It was their second Final Four appearance during Todd's four years at IU. Unfortunately, they never won a championship together. Photo: Robb Hill, 1995 *Arbutus.*

from their children to the players and administrators. "There's no law or rule of thumb in life that says that your spouse, your partner, or your closest people to you are going to help you or be a great part of your success," Don Rawson said. "There are some people I'm sure that could or would do it on their own. He would have been successful by himself, but he is more loved and respected because of the team they are and always have been. He enjoys and embraces the fact that Marilyn is a big part of what he does. She supports what he does as a coach and is his biggest cheerleader."

"It was a stroke of genius to get me involved," Marilyn said. "I think he just wanted me there. I don't think he had a game plan. It was never premeditated. It just happened, and it happened beautifully. 'Why shouldn't my wife be sharing in my thought process? Why shouldn't she be involved in what I'm doing?' It's so joyful when things go right. We can share when things don't go so right. If you don't share that with someone, what's the whole point? And that's why he involved the kids as much as possible."

The Yeagleys are the heart and soul of IU soccer. Over the years, they have reached out to hundreds and thousands of people—players, fans, camp staff, band members. Everyone who is touched by the program becomes part of the IU soccer family.

Reaching Out

When Jerry Yeagley took over the IU men's soccer program, the players began to do everything together, and soon they came to think of each other as family. Yeagley served as a father figure to many. He was there to give advice, to give hugs, and to be stern when that was needed. Marilyn enjoyed mothering the team. She could always be counted on to brighten up the players' days with a warm smile, a hug, and some cookies. They always had a home away from home, and they knew they were not alone. The same goes for the assistant coaches and support staff. They had a bond not just on the field, but off it as well. And that bond will last a lifetime. "You know you're in it, the soccer family, the moment that Jerry, Marilyn, Todd, or Yvette reaches out to you," broadcaster Chris Doran said. "And it doesn't take long. He will reach out to you on some level at some point if he senses your interest—and through some of the simplest things will make you feel very important."

"Family's always been a part of it," Yeagley said. "That maybe stems back to the club days, where we had to do everything together. We had to do it to survive. We'd stop and eat at homes of players. We had our own cars. We didn't have all the support services that varsity sports provide. We've continued some of those traditions, some of those things that athletes in other sports would say they don't do."

Jerry and Marilyn spent four years watching boys turn into men. They cared about the players on and off the field. And

Always the father figure, Coach Yeagley comforts reserve goalkeeper Doug Warren in the locker room in 1999. Photo: JJ Canull.

they knew everything about these students. They knew their families, their girlfriends, and their goals. The Yeagleys helped the players in every way they could. "He refers to the players as sons," Marilyn said. "You don't give up on family. You don't give up on siblings. That's why he never left this level. He felt this is what he was meant to do."

The players further describe Yeagley as a mentor, a friend, and a polished and distinguished gentleman. He taught them a lot about life, and along the way, everything he did was done with class. From the moment the players met him, they were in awe of his deep voice and commanding presence. But within a few minutes, he made them feel like one of his. "When Coach Yeagley first came to see me, he came to a tournament in St. Louis," Chris Klein said. "In walks Coach

Yeagley in a long blue adidas trench coat, with the assistant coaches on either side. It was almost as if the whole place stopped and stared in awe."

Once the players felt comfortable with Coach, they met the rest of the family. Marilyn welcomed each of them to the IU soccer family. She treated everyone the same way, from a new freshman to a fifth-year senior. "Coach is the guy that built Indiana soccer," Klein said, "but Mrs. Yeags is instrumental in making you feel at home. All the coaches and their wives really care about you as a person and your family."

Every IU player who participated in a College Cup experienced a unique Thanksgiving with their second family. "If we're not having Thanksgiving dinner together as a team, it hasn't been a successful year," Yeagley said. "That means we're out

Coach Yeagley jokes with players Danny O'Rourke and Ned Grabavoy at a pregame meal in 2003. Photo: Chris Howell, *The Herald-Times*.

of the tournament early. If we're having Thanksgiving dinner together, we're making the push for the Final Four." In the beginning, Jerry and Marilyn hosted the holiday gathering at their home. In later years, the team dressed up and went to the Tudor Room in the Union for a feast.

One of the unique qualities of the Hoosier soccer family is that the closeness doesn't end when the players leave IU. Yeagley spoke to his former players on a daily basis. Both they and their families stayed in touch with Jerry and Marilyn and the staff. They called Yeagley for advice, and he called them to see how they were doing. "The whole IU soccer family starts with the Yeagleys," Rhett Tauber said. "We had no idea the organization was set up the way it was. They are wonderful people and made everyone feel right at home."

The Tailgate

In the early days, the players and their families would meet at the Yeagleys' house after every game to celebrate the day's events. After the NCAA established new regulations, everyone had to find a new place to gather. Slowly but surely, the IU soccer tailgate was born. Those tailgates are now legendary, and the envy of teams across the country. "Our home was their home after every home game," Marilyn said. "It lent itself to the closeness that we had not only with the players, but with the parents, and the players getting to know other parents. I feel that after it was no longer possible to do that, the tailgates took over. 'We can't go to Yeagleys', but we're all together. We're outside. It may be freezing. It may be raining. We've got the brats going. We have the beer in the tub. We're still getting together.' This made the program even stronger."

The idea originated with Denny and Peggy Stalter, who run the Trojan Horse and Athletics International. They helped

out with camp every year, and one year assistant coach Mike Freitag asked them if they knew of any way to get more people into the stands. The Stalters suggested a tailgate, and so it began in 1997. "I was grilling, had a cooler set up, and was waiting for some of my friends to show up," Denny Stalter said. "The Fadeskis roared into the parking lot. Dennis pulls up, parks, looks at me, and asks for a beer and asks what I was doing. I told him I was waiting for friends to tailgate. He said, 'This isn't a tailgate.' He said the next week he would bring his supplies, because he had been tailgating with the Packers for years. That's how we got started."

Soon the tailgate was the place to be before games. A tent covered the food spread. Brats were grilled and beverages poured. "Teams that we played just marveled at our tailgates," Sue Tauber said. "It was easier to get to know the parents at tailgates. It was a way to break the ice with the new parents."

Anyone wearing IU apparel was invited to join in. Dennis "Papa Bear" Fadeski and portable Packer Man made sure to greet everyone with a handshake or a hug. Fadeski was the original host, but after his son graduated, others stepped in to help welcome newcomers. "The soccer tailgate is an institution in and of itself," Associate Athletic Director Amelia Noël said. "It doesn't matter if a son is on the team or isn't. Parents are still there. The people who run the tailgates are incredible and friendly. It's a fun experience that travels across the country." "It's such a great tradition," Nancy Chirico added. "Whether you contribute or not, everyone is welcome. It doesn't matter if it's a home game or not. We bring out the cookers, put out the spread, raise the flag, and tailgate."

Perhaps the best thing about the tailgate is that it travels with the team. Wherever the team goes, the tailgate follows. In 1999, the Hoosiers traveled to Char-

Parents gathered for a tailgate. Dennis "Papa Bear" Fadeski and Denny Stalter began the tradition in 1997. Photo: The Stalters.

lotte, North Carolina, for the NCAA Championships. The parking lot of the stadium was not really conducive to tailgating, so the parents found a new place to set up. "In Charlotte, there was not enough room in the parking lot," Papa Bear Fadeski said. "We went across the street to a steel yard and asked the guy if we could have our tailgate there. The IUAA had a tailgate across the street. Ours was so successful that they packed theirs up and joined us."

People often say that in addition to recruiting the best players, the IU coaches recruit the best parents. "We were at a tailgate before IU took a trip to California," Erin Fadeski said. "Coach asked how many parents were going, and everyone started to say, 'I'm going' and raised their hands. Coach said, 'I've never had this many parents travel.' Ninety percent of the parents traveled for three years. It's a family."

The soccer tailgate is yet another reflection of the history that Indiana soccer has created. "The program is a history of relationships," performance coach Rob Kehoe said. "The emphasis so often is that players are there to build the program. At IU, the program is a means of building people. The tailgates say a lot about the family atmosphere. They're basically family picnics."

The IU Experience

Picture this: The stadium is packed with fans decked out in red and white or cream and crimson. They sit on both sides of the stadium, and some stand around the fence. A few are shirtless, with messages written across their chests. The IU cheerleaders are lined up on the track surrounding the field. The band sits in the middle of the stands, belting out songs that excite the crowd. The team runs onto the field. The Crabb Band begins to play the IU Fight Song. The spectators rise as one and clap along with the tune. Welcome to the IU experience!

The Crabb Band, named after Associ-

ate Athletic Director Chuck Crabb, performs at every home game. The band members attend the tailgates and lead cheers in the stands. They play fan favorites that are guaranteed to get everyone up on their feet. "We have such great fans," Crabb Band director Will Petersen said. "It's really easy to get them into the spirit of the game. There is an extended family, and everyone is working for a common goal."

Occasionally the band gets to take a road trip. In the 2003 season, the IU Foundation and a friend of the program arranged for the band to travel to UCLA. They literally took over the stands. And in 1998, a few band members jumped in a van and drove to Clemson, South Carolina, to root the Hoosiers on against the Tigers. They went on their own just to show support for the team. "We started walking through the tunnel and singing the IU Fight Song," former band member Mike Simons said. "We saw Coach Yeagley. He met us with a huge grin. The team applauded us and we applauded them."

Former band member John Koluder remembers that day fondly. "We staked our claim in the corner," Koluder said. "The rest of the IU fans joined us. We were there being loud and proud. It's great to hear players talk about how it feels like a home game when we're there. We're doing our part and doing what we can to help. We're kind of adding the extra spark."

The band members become loyal supporters of IU soccer. "I remember sitting at games with parents," Simons said. "They let us become part of their community. To think that would happen with football or basketball is ludicrous. It was just phenomenal."

The cheerleaders, too, are a part of the IU soccer experience. "I remember in '76 when we first played SIU to go to the Final Four, we showed up and the cheerleaders were there," said Scott Rosen, the first varsity manager. "We thought, what?

Cheerleaders at a soccer game? We weren't used to it. At that time, the rest of the population that hadn't come out to watch soccer became interested."

Camp Memories

In the summer, boys and girls from around the country travel to Bloomington to attend the IU soccer camp. Coaches from across the nation come to coach the children. Yeagley oversaw everything during his years at IU, while Marilyn organized the event. She developed a system that enabled everything to be handled very professionally. As children, Todd and Yvette also spent their summers at camp. "I looked so forward to camp," Yvette said. "In December my Mom started sending out flyers for camp. It was fun to be there every day. Guys who coached camp loved it. It was like a family every summer. There are so many stories about soccer camp. Those were some of the most fun times I had as a kid."

IU's soccer camp is nationally recognized as one of the best in the nation. It's a memorable experience for everyone involved, from the campers to the coaches. "I grew up coming here and admiring the people in the red shirts," camp counselor Mandy Madden said. "I put on a shirt and got teary-eyed. It's an amazing honor working under Coach Yeagley."

The coaches who come to camp are aware of IU's tradition and family and want to be a part of it. "It's impressive that a program stayed so good for so long with one person behind everything," Bucknell assistant coach and camp coach Brian Suskiewicz said. "It says volumes about what kind of person Coach Yeagley is."

Camp is yet another branch of the ever-growing IU soccer tree. "The soccer family is just one of those things you almost have to see and experience to believe," Sean Phillips said. "You see it at conventions. You see it at camp. Some of the peo-

Facing page: IU soccer fans are as loyal as they come. They will bear (and sometimes bare!) anything to root their team on to victory. Photo: Kathryn Griffin, 2004 *Arbutus.*

ple that are part of it are Coach's friends who've been in Bloomington for years. It's a commonality of a desire for excellence the right way, without cutting corners to make it over the long haul. I don't think it's an accident that almost everybody who is a part of it has qualities that are special."

For forty-one years, the IU soccer family has grown with every game. The players appreciate the support they receive, and the fans appreciate the games and the joy of winning. "IU has by far the best fans and the best tailgating," Nick Garcia said. "It's unbelievable. We play in one of the premier soccer stadiums in the country, with tons of IU fans. We have a great following. Without fans we'd be playing for ourselves. They get spoiled. They've enjoyed it as much as we have."

Two of IU's most loyal fans, Nancy Hayworth and Charlie Teeple, attended every home match. Teeple became interested in the soccer program after he retired. "I was interested in following something that had a winning tradition," he said. Teeple and his wife traveled around the country to see the Hoosiers play, unless they had a prior family obligation. "IU soccer is my number one hobby. It's been great for meeting a high-quality group of people. And it's provided me with some wonderful trips. IU soccer is a family tradition with a very friendly atmosphere."

Hayworth began attending IU soccer

matches in 1979. In twenty-five years, she missed only five home games. "My dedication to the team really has to do with the quality of people involved in the program. They care about each other and care about everyone involved with the program. No matter what your connection to the team is, you were part of the IU soccer family. You were part of a really elite group of people."

Many things changed around Bloomington in Yeagley's forty-one years as IU's men's soccer coach, but one thing stayed the same: If you wanted to watch a quality sporting event and leave the stadium feeling good, you went to a soccer game. You watched the team dominate opponents, and you shared in the joy of being part of one of the elite programs in the nation. The next generation of IU coaches plans to maintain the tradition. "When you have this father figure there for so long, it makes it a lot easier," Todd said. "One of our challenges as he moves on is to keep it as a family atmosphere. I think with who we have here, we can do that. We have enough respect for the tradition and know what has happened here. My dad has been the one central figure. Creating a family is something he's done and maintained. A huge part of that has been my mom's influence as well." Despite Jerry Yeagley's departure, the IU soccer family is here to stay.

3

The Heart of the Hoosier

The heart of the Hoosier. Either you have it or you don't. When new soccer players arrive in Bloomington, they quickly begin to feel that they belong. They have been invited to join a winning program and to strive to take it to the ultimate level. When they put on their cream and crimson adidas uniforms for the first time and enter Bill Armstrong Stadium to the cheers of fans and cheerleaders and to tunes from the Crabb Band, they become part of the IU tradition. They honor and respect the uniform and the school, and when times get tough, they keep their composure. They play one game at a time and rely on the heart of the Hoosier to carry them through difficult moments. And after they finish their years at IU, they take valuable lessons with them on whatever path they choose. The heart of the Hoosier beats permanently in each former player. "It's something that you can't coach," Danny O'Rourke said. "You can't coach heart or train heart. All the coaches recruit players that they know have heart. They may not be the flashiest

Tyler Hawley stares out the window as the team travels to the 1999 NCAA semifinal game vs. UCLA. IU won the match 3-2 in quadruple sudden-death overtime. Photo: Chris Howell, *The Herald-Times.*

Lazo Alavanja, Yuri Lavrinenko, and Caleb Porter congratulate Nick Garcia at the 1997 Big Ten Championships. Garcia tallied the lone goal for the Hoosiers in their 1-0 victory over Ohio State in the championship game. Photo: Dmitry Kiyatkin, 1998 *Arbutus*.

players, the best athletes, or the best players. But the coaches always recruit players who have heart and the will to win. I think that's what's made us so successful. We have the heart, and we always want to win. We can't be counted out of any game."

Finding the Heart

The coaches look for certain characteristics in prospective players. They want winners with heart, players who will give it their all and never give up. "The coaching staff recruits guys who take great pride in winning," Ned Grabavoy said. "There is absolutely no way we will accept defeat. We'll do whatever it takes to win, all in fair play and underneath a very classy coach." A lot of athletes have heart; it's in their nature. But the key is relying on that heart when things get tough. That's when the heart of the Hoosier beats strong.

At the beginning of the 2003 season, the Hoosiers' prospects looked dim. The team endured a grueling first nine games, with disappointing results. But the players persevered, and they found a way to prevail. "The talent level of college players is usually so close that what separates Indiana from the rest of college soccer is our ability to handle pressure and our heart," O'Rourke said. "That was shown when we played Penn State and were down 2-0. A lot of teams without as much heart as we have would have given up at 2-0. With a record of 2-3-4, a lot of teams would have disappeared. But at IU, everyone expects greatness. We had a lot of heart on our team this year. And we fought every day in practice to improve. In every game we fought to win."

Finding the Key

Once the coaches have recruited players with heart, they must find the right spot for each in the lineup. Every player brings

different qualities to a team. Yeagley and his staff tended to look for speedy athletes, especially forwards. Many of the players that Yeagley recruited played forward in high school, but at Indiana he found a different place for them on the field. Some of his top defenders had never played a defensive position until arriving at IU. "In high school, all the good players are forwards," Tyler Hawley said. "They're scoring all the goals. You don't see anyone stopping them. Coach Yeagley recruits athletes and forwards. If you look at our runs, we're so much more athletic and fit than anyone in the country. Plus, we have players with a little bit of attitude. Practice sessions are even harder than game settings because everyone wants to win. Everyone's at each other's heels trying to make a starting spot."

Once players are placed in the lineup, Yeagley evaluates their skills and assesses what it takes to motivate them. "He's the master of reading people to get the most out of them," Assistant Coach Mike Freitag said. "He knows which players you need to pat on the butt and which ones you need to kick in the butt. I think that's a key to coaching. He gets people to play to their potential and feel good about themselves, finding out what makes them tick."

"I've never motivated anyone," Yeagley said. "The challenge is to find a way for the individual to have self-motivation, to find what will drive them and push them to their potential. We try to provide that environment and encourage them to want to be their best—find the key." Once the players are motivated, the next step is to fit each piece into the puzzle.

Fitting into the Puzzle

After finding the key to a new player, the coaches decide where to place him on the field. At the beginning of the season, the team may not yet have strong chemistry, but once all the pieces fit together, they begin to succeed. "The coaches have a system they stick to, no matter what," Gino DiGuardi said. "It's easily outlined, and you understand the role you're given. Either you do the job that your position requires, or someone else will. Everybody buys into the system."

Yeagley believes that his ability to find the right position for each player is a big part of his success: "For every coach, the X's and O's don't separate who's successful or not. We all know the game. We all know how to teach the techniques. What separates those who succeed from those who don't, given the same talent, is almost an instinct for knowing how to put together an effective unit, knowing what roles to give to players and how to achieve the most effective unit. You can have eleven very gifted players, and unless they're placed on the field properly and given the proper roles, it may not be a very effective unit. You can also have eleven very gifted players, but in the mix of workers and artists, piano players and piano carriers, you need some soldiers, you need some workers. You may need to take two or three of those gifted ones out of there and put in some role players to get the right mix. I felt I always had that instinct, that I knew how to put an effective unit on the field."

Instinct definitely paid off for the Hoosiers. The competition was so fierce that some players didn't make it onto the field. It wasn't easy to sit on the bench, watching others succeed and wishing that you could be out there, but many players chose sitting on the bench at Indiana over starting at another school. "I turned down scholarships to come to IU and try to walk on," John Swann said. "I didn't want to settle for hills. I wanted to climb the highest mountain. I wanted to actually do good. I didn't just want to settle for just playing."

Jordan Chirico shared those sentiments: "When I came to IU, I made the decision that even if I didn't play for a year, I was still going to play here. Either way I was going to become a better player. If I went somewhere else and started every game, I might not be a better player. It's the quality of playing here. If others are better than you are, then they should be on the field. The coaches do it fairly."

IU had many regulars in the starting lineups over the years, but the starting positions were not guaranteed. Each player had to earn a spot. And once he earned it, he had to fight to keep it. "They've always been the best in high school. They come to Indiana and are no longer the best," said Scott Jones, Coach Yeagley's son-in-law. "It's so competitive. It's tough when you expect to be a superstar but sit on the bench. Do you want to be a superstar on a decent team or a part of a great team? Guys are willing to do that to be a part of IU."

Certain players are called into the game specifically to pick things up, either offensively or defensively. They may not be starters, they may not play in every game, but if they work hard, they get noticed. And they get called upon to help in the rough times. "Coach Yeagley really gets attached to the guys that have been there and done it," Ernie Yarborough said. "He calls them the salty dogs. They come in, do their job, don't say a word, and get the job done. They work hard. They earn everything they get."

Players who didn't see much playing time remained as loyal to the program as anyone. "I never really played," Sean Phillips said. "I was a reserve goalkeeper. If you're the seventh best midfielder, you're going to get to play. But if you're the second best goalkeeper, you're not. So I left after three years pretty happy with things. That's probably one of the unique things. I've had friends at other soccer programs that were in similar scenarios as far as not playing a lot. They have a bitter taste from their experience. I don't. The non-stars or the reserves, they're just as supportive of the program as some of the starters. It is pretty unique and a testament to how Coach Yeagley treats people." Yeagley always included everyone in the program. IU could not have had a successful season without the participation of each and every player. After all, everyone who suits up in the cream and crimson becomes a part of IU history.

Players pave their own way at Indiana and determine their own fate. In games or at practice, they must compete to the best of their ability, playing with heart, playing with fight, playing honestly, and keeping their standards high.

Keeping High Standards

Once players earned a spot on the field, it wasn't always easy to keep it. The competition was intense. You had to play by the rules and give it your all every day. No cheating. No cutting corners. You had to go in and compete to the best of your ability. "We've always kept standards high in practice and in games," Coach Freitag said. "We're always shooting for perfection. We'll never get there. But you always hold those standards up there to try. Our expectation every year is to make it to the College Cup, win the Big Ten, and get in that final. But that takes a whole lot of work. There's a lot of sacrifice."

Players knew what was expected of them. They learned their positions. But they had to keep their individual standards high as well. They had to perform up to the expectations of the coaching staff, or they would find themselves watching from the sidelines. Yeagley said he always looked for honest players, the ones who gave 100 percent or more all of the time. "I don't have a lot of room for players who cheat on the field, take shortcuts, don't do their part," Yeagley said. "There have been very gifted players who sat the bench until they got that way, or if they didn't,

they didn't play much. That's one of the biggest challenges in coaching. A lot of time, your marquis players were allowed to take breaks on their high school teams and not defend and not do the unpleasant things. When they come to college, to us, it comes as a bit of a shock. It's a bit of a fight, a tug of war, to see if we'll allow a lot of that to continue. I won't say I don't expect the same amount from everyone, but the min-imal amount has to be higher. There has to be a certain standard."

Indiana soccer is always played with respect and class. That is a standard looked up to by many. Yeagley's teams knew how

Coach Yeagley celebrates a moment with his players during the 1988 season. Photo: Todd Anderson, 1989 *Arbutus*.

to be classy in victory and graceful in defeat. "The thing that people love about Indiana soccer is the way we play with respect for the other team," Jay Nolly said. "We're not a dirty team. We just play our hearts out. I think that's something Coach Yeagley stresses. Even if we're losing, we're not going to be a dirty team."

Although IU may have played clean year after year, the Hoosiers were still the team to beat. There were soccer powerhouses across the country—Virginia, UCLA, St. Louis, San Francisco—but on any given day, IU could tangle with the best of them. "You were the best of the best wherever you went. Wherever you play, everybody is out to beat you," Scott Coufal said. "You're looked at as the team that sets the bar for college soccer. If you're playing for Indiana soccer, people look at you in awe."

Taking Pride in Tradition

Yeagley always believed that players wearing the IU uniform were representing more than just the team and the extended soccer family. "Take pride in the uniform," Yeagley said. "Take pride in the colors. When you take the field, feel that tingle in your skin that you're wearing the IU colors. You're representing not only yourself, but also your school and the responsibility that goes with it, pride and honor. It's a privilege. You have a certain responsibility when you have that uniform on to more than just yourself. We've established that tradition with the program over the years."

It takes years to form a tradition. Even in the early club days, Yeagley impressed upon his players the importance of representing Indiana soccer. He made everyone feel a part of the program, as long as they understood what the tradition stood for. "When he showed up in Bloomington, he had a car and a dream," Ernie Yarborough said. "He wanted to be a soccer coach. Obviously he was working for the university, but he wanted to become a soccer coach. He built it all. And more than anything, it's been done the right way so that you feel a part of it."

Everyone truly is a part of it. The players from the '70s have much in common with players from the '90s. They all know and understand what it means to put on an IU uniform. They all share war stories and reminisce about the good old days. They all bleed cream and crimson. "There is something extra inside of you that pushes you to take it a step further than anyone else can take it," Scott Coufal said. "Something that pushed me to the next level was the fact that I was playing for myself, but I was also playing for Coach Yeagley, all my teammates, and all the former players that have ever played at Indiana. When you put on that Indiana uniform, whether it's for a game or a practice, you are held to a higher level of responsibility than at any other program in the country. I think Coach Yeagley also looks for a certain type of player to play at Indiana."

Yeagley made sure that everyone who suited up in an IU uniform understood the challenges the program had endured. The players learned about the championship years and the years when the team fell short. They could name past players and look up to them with the utmost respect. "Coach Yeagley is very good at letting the players know that the alumni paved the way for them," Caleb Porter said. "He always introduces alumni to the players and talks about how good they were and how they helped to pave your way. He wants the current players not to take for granted the early years and how that helped get the program to where it is today."

The pressure of representing a tradition can be intense. "I can still remember my first official game as a freshman," Mike

Clark said. "My family was there. I was nervous. You know who wore the number before you. On my first touch, I turned to pass it back to our keeper. I hit it so hard, he had to make a diving save. That's how excited I was."

Marilyn Yeagley managed to get inside the locker room after IU won the 2003 championship. She had never been in the locker room before. Coach Yeagley in-troduced Pat McGauley, a former player who now works for Anheuser-Busch, to the team, mentioning that McGauley had brought free beer for everyone. Marilyn Yeagley: "The players were ecstatic. All of a sudden Jerry said, 'Can someone tell me what Pat McGauley . . .' Ned Grabavoy spoke up and said he had the winning goal in 1983 and won the championship. For that present player to know what that

Dan King and goalkeeper Bruce Killough sit on the bench in disbelief after the Hoosiers' 2-1 loss to the Clemson Tigers in the 1984 NCAA title game. Photo: Jim Greenwood, 1985 *Arbutus.*

past player . . . it warmed my heart. Jerry is doing this so right. Every player who has gone through the program knows what past players have done, the struggles that took place in the club years. And I said this is why it's so successful. He doesn't allow any team to go by without letting them know the past. In order to be successful in the present, you really do need to know the importance of wearing the jersey. It's something so innate about Jerry. It's something he may not even realize. It's just that he loves to share stories."

Every player becomes a part of the IU soccer tradition. But it's not just the players who have contributed to that tradition. Yeagley, his fellow coaches, and his support staff all played a part in making IU soccer one of the powerhouses in the country. And Yeagley did it the right way, by surrounding himself with successful people.

Surrounding Yourself with Success

In Jerry Yeagley's forty-one years of coaching, soccer changed tremendously. Yet one thing that stayed the same was success at Indiana. Players came and players went, but every year, the Hoosiers succeeded. From back in the club days to 2003, success was synonymous with Indiana soccer. "Coach Yeagley is always looking to grow with the game," Coach Freitag said. "When you're in the game forty-one years, a lot of things are going to change. Coach has been very smart in the sense that he has stayed on top of the game, trends. He has surrounded himself with good people over the years. To be successful and have a good program, you have to have everything in the right place."

Yeagley not only stressed that success was required, he surrounded himself with the best of the best to make that happen. From the academic counselors to the trainers to the assistant coaches to his own

family, everyone was a part of the success. And Yeagley gave credit where credit was due. "I love seeing him around his coaching staff," head strength coach Katrin Koch said. "He's so open to their opinions. I've never seen a staff discuss things more. They'll argue for a half-hour until it's game time. When it comes time, he makes the smartest choice. Sometimes he sticks by his guns, and other times he goes with the other opinion. Obviously, it's paid off big-time."

Yeagley surrounded himself with assistant coaches who not only knew the game but were also fierce competitors. They might have been head coaches elsewhere in the league. "He's been so blessed with great coaching, great coaches," Marilyn Yeagley said. "His assistants have been remarkable. I like his attitude and his coaching style, where on paper he might be the head coach, but in reality they're all head coaches. The input that would come from an assistant or even a volunteer coach was as important as anything. He took that to heart. He would mull it over. He was never afraid to make changes and then give credit where credit was due."

The assistant coaches themselves agreed that Yeagley was fair as a head coach. He listened to their opinions before weighing the options, and they then made decisions together. "A lot of us assistant coaches played here," George Perry said. "We understood his system. We understood his coaching. I can remember having fierce battles about how we were going to play and who would play. But when we walked out the door, once the decision was made, you walked out as one. He always had the final say. He taught you that you always had the opportunity to voice your opinions."

Winning is a huge part of the Hoosier soccer tradition, but so is respect. "Coach has qualities that lend themselves to winning," Don Rawson said. "I don't know if

it's always about winning. I know he is all about being successful. I think part of being successful is winning. But he was about more than that. He was about succeeding with dignity and succeeding in being fair, succeeding within the rules, succeeding with a smile, succeeding and everybody knowing they're part of it and sharing in the accolades. It wasn't about him, it was about all those around him." The qualities that Yeagley impressed on his players throughout the years showed on the field, but many remained with the players off the field as well.

Influencing Lives

Yeagley served as a mentor, a friend, a father, a brother, and much more for many of his players. He became a huge part of their lives in very impressionable years. He let his players know that he would always be there for them. "The influence you have on this age is the biggest reason my dad

has stayed in this arena," Todd Yeagley said. "You can have a huge impact on their lives in soccer and out of soccer. It's a special four years that you have with the players. You're much more of a mentor at this age."

Professional teams courted Yeagley to take his coaching to the next level, but he never left IU. He had a love for the university, a love for the students, and a love for helping adolescents become men. He always wanted to be a teacher and a coach, and he succeeded in both capacities. "He's a teacher," daughter Yvette Jones said. "At the professional level, you don't have the same mentoring dynamic. The young guys who came in as kids left as adults. He loved working with an age where you're able to make a mark. I don't think he ever wanted to lose the dynamic. I don't think he ever wanted to get involved with the professional side of sport, the big business. He truly loves being a teacher."

Justin Tauber, Ryan Hammer, and T. J. Hannig spend time signing autographs and visiting with fans at the "Afternoon with Champions" in 1999. Fans came out in numbers to congratulate the team after the Hoosiers won their fifth NCAA Championship. Photo: Chris Howell, *The Herald-Times.*

Many of Yeagley's players came back to Bloomington to coach beside him. Many came in as volunteer coaches who wanted to learn coaching strategies from the man who had inspired them. In that situation, Yeagley would become a mentor instead of a coach. "The relationship was now teacher-student—more on the lines of mentor," Ernie Yarborough said. "He'd ask questions, you'd give answers. He would question you to think about the reasons for your answers. He most often knew the answer, but he would help you figure it out for yourself. He would listen to what you say."

Yeagley taught his players countless lessons. But most important were the skills he taught them for succeeding in everyday life. When players look back on their days at Indiana, they realize that there was a lesson in almost everything they did. "After every road game we'd go to Wendy's," Mike Clark said. "I always noticed Coach would let everyone eat before he got anything to eat himself. When we were at the airport, he made sure everyone's bags were taken care of and everyone was checked in before he checked in. Typically it's the opposite. I wrote Coach a letter and thanked him for let-

Coach Yeagley follows his team down the corridor for the last time during the 2003 regular season as they take the field for the second period of the game against Penn State on November 8th. Photo: Chris Howell, *The Herald-Times.*

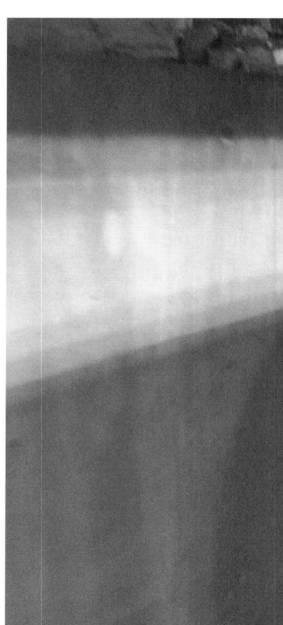

ting me eat first. Great leaders make sure that everyone's taken care of before they take care of themselves."

Yeagley's lessons touched more lives than just his players'. Most of the people he met in his years at IU could tell you a similar story. When Yeagley's daughter-in-law, Suzy Yeagley, spoke at his retirement roast in February 2004, she got a buzz from the crowd. "We took a shuttle to the roast," Suzy began. "We were all riding on the bus. Everyone got off the bus, and Coach was still sitting there. I asked him if he was going to get off the bus. He said, 'I'm always the last person off the bus.' That's when I realized that he's always behind us. At one point or another, he's been behind everyone in this room."

Yeagley spent forty-one years learning what it took to make players tick and how to get the most out of everyone who took the field. He coached with class, patience, and dignity. His players left with lessons that would last a lifetime. Yeagley's players had heart. And the heart of the Hoosier still beats in each and every one of them.

4

The Pre-Varsity Years

When Jerry Yeagley arrived at Indiana University, he became a teacher in the School of Health, Physical Education, and Recreation. His other task was to coach the men's soccer club and to build it into a varsity team. From the first day he met with the core of the squad, he knew that would be a challenge. To them it seemed to be more of a social club.

But Yeagley soon showed them the bigger picture—winning.

Yeagley Arrives

Formed in 1947, the club team had been fairly successful. When Yeagley arrived in 1963, he had a new outlook: It was time to turn this club team into a varsity team. He then embarked upon a huge task, ini-

The 1963 club team photo. The team had a 6-1-3 record in its debut under Coach Yeagley. Photo: Yeagley collection.

tiating some immediate changes. First of all, he was no longer the club's supervisor; he was the new team's coach. "I didn't treat it as if I was supervisor," Yeagley said. "I treated it as I'm going to coach this group of guys and we're not going to just call ourselves a club, we're going to be a team—the Indiana University soccer team."

One of the first tasks was to make some rules. Eligibility would be a huge factor. If the team was going to appeal for varsity status, it had to play by the varsity rules. The earlier teams had included graduate students, but only undergraduates would be suiting up under Yeagley. "My goal right from the start, and I was encouraged along these lines, was simple," he said. "If you want to become varsity, you need to start operating in a varsity structure. We did this right from the beginning."

It took a while for the returning club team to adapt to the new rules. When Yeagley got to Bloomington, he called the captain from the year before and arranged a meeting. The captain, in turn, called a number of returning players. The eight of them met with Yeagley in a quaint room in the HPER building. Yeagley was surprised when they asked him, "Where will we travel this year?"

"It seemed like the most important question they had was what were the trips for the year," Yeagley said. "They were very interested in what good parties they were going to go to. The social aspect in the past had been a big part of it. I think rugby and soccer clubs were truly the social clubs. This was a bit of a shock to me because I came from a very structured, disciplined college program where everybody was very serious. I realized it was going to be a bit of a challenge. I just started putting one foot in front of the other and trying to get the guys to become more serious about developing the program, and the team working toward

varsity status. It was a bit of a tug-of-war at first with the fellas. As we realized success early on, they bought in."

Yeagley's enthusiasm was contagious. It was a new beginning for the club team. The players began to focus on fitness. Everyone started catching the soccer bug—and winning. When you string together a couple of wins, you gain the confidence you need to get out there and give it your all.

The Adventure Begins

Yeagley knew that the club team would be a challenge, but he may not have known just how challenging it would be. He had no staff to help him out; this was a one-man show until he married Marilyn, and then it became a two-person show. Yeagley oversaw everything. And he, Marilyn, and the team did everything themselves. They lined fields, put up goalposts, and washed their own uniforms. (In the early days, they wore old football jerseys.) They dug rocks out of Woodlawn Field. The players advertised their games in any way possible, from painting announcements on bed sheets and hanging them on buildings to going to the fraternities and sororities to announce their upcoming events. "We had limited resources and limited abilities," Jeff Richardson said. "We had no scholarships, no real field, no support. We still had a great time and really learned to love soccer even more. Under those conditions, you'd have to love soccer."

When Richardson first joined the club team and Yeagley took him to get his equipment, "I thought it would be packaged in a box," Richardson said. "We went up to an attic area. There were literally huge boxes, one box shorts, one box shirts, one box shin guards (either bamboo or cheap plastic in various states of disrepair), one box socks, one box jock straps, one box shoes (most of them used) and yellow and red practice jerseys. I took

No. 23." Richardson didn't mind the lack of luxuries. "Everything was great. I was so excited. I was on cloud nine to be able to play soccer in college as I did in high school."

It may not have been what the players had dreamed that playing soccer in college would be like, but they enjoyed their experiences regardless. They look back fondly on the club days. "We didn't look at it like it was a negative thing," Don Rawson said. "We hung sheets on campus about when the games were, put posters on telephone poles and pieces of paper underneath every door on campus. We took our own cars on road trips and things like that. There wasn't a budget for meals; you did your own thing."

The players mounted their own public relations campaign, doing everything they could think of to get people interested in coming to their games. "We were doing everything ourselves," Gary Fresen said. "We had our own little treasury. We made posters, handouts, and brochures. It was a real grassroots kind of effort." And it worked—the fans poured in to cheer the Hoosiers on and spend an evening with their friends. "We had thousands of people come out," added Fresen. "We had the third-largest spectator sport after football and basketball."

In those early years, the players had to drive their own cars to games. They often joked that if you had a car, you traveled. They would often stop to eat meals with each other's families. Some of those meals became legendary. "There have been lots of great adventures," Bob Rossow said. "Once a year when we played a game in Ft. Wayne, we'd stop off at the Jensens' home on the way back. They were a Swedish family. Their mother and the family would prepare this spread. And it was gooood! We all looked forward tremendously to our meal at the Jensens'."

Yeagley, too, looks back on the club days with a smile. "Some of my most fond memories are from the club days," Yeagley said. "We had to do everything. I remember driving my own car. And my wife changing diapers in the car with players in the back seat. I remember Marilyn washing uniforms and us lining our own fields. We basically did everything. The club guys worked hard generating interest. They'd go to the dorms handing out schedules and flyers. They'd hang up sheets about our games, bed sheets. I never asked where they got them, but they came up with bed sheets. They'd hang them in the trees or on buildings announcing our games."

"The club years are the funniest, the most frustrating, the most demanding, the most time-consuming," Marilyn Yeagley said. "They took so much more energy than being involved with the team today. Ignorance is bliss, and youth is great. If you believe in something, you try to make it happen."

The foundation of the IU soccer family was laid in the club days. Those early teams worked for everything they got, both on and off the field. In the process, they gained the respect of others around them. Soon more people were watching soccer at IU than were watching baseball, swimming, or track.

The Players

Every IU undergraduate male student was eligible to be part of the club team. The players came in all shapes, sizes, and nationalities. Yeagley was willing to give everyone a chance. His teams were a combination of international students who had played soccer all their lives and American students who had no knowledge of the game. "We had a very interesting mix of players," Yeagley said. "In those days, there were a lot of international undergraduates on campus, and some very good soccer players. We had, on one hand, a handful of experienced internationals, and on the other hand, we had guys who I invited to come out for the club who were in PE classes I taught. They were good athletes, but some had never kicked a soccer ball. Most of the guys that signed up for the soccer class hadn't played much at all. We had a few from the East that had played in high school. Around here, none of the schools played. You couldn't even buy a soccer ball in Bloomington. We had quite an ingenious mix of experience and ability."

Yeagley took his variety of players and found places for all of them. "Most of the hard-nosed athletes who hadn't played a lot of soccer played the defensive roles," Yeagley said. "The internationals were pretty much the midfielders and attackers."

Every practice was a challenge. Yeagley emphasized the basics of the game. He did his best to mold the mix of athletes and soccer players into a team, but it wasn't always easy. And the players will be the first to tell you that they didn't play the prettiest soccer. But if you want to win, you have to find a way. "We were well-conditioned and well-drilled," Bob Rossow said. "We would defeat the opposition by wearing them down. We were intimidating because some of our players were football players in high school and were quite large."

Yeagley looks back on the club days as some of his most rewarding years. Here he was, taking athletes who had never touched a soccer ball and turning them into soccer players. A prime example of the success he achieved is a man by the name of Bob Cooley. Cooley originally came to IU to play football, but after being told that he was too small, he began hanging around soccer practice. One day Yeagley asked one of his players, who was a friend of Cooley's, who this guy was and why he was just standing there. Coach then invited Cooley to come out

and train with the team. Five years later, Bob Cooley joined the Cincinnati Comets and became the first African American to play professional soccer in the United States. "He never kicked a ball until he was eighteen years old," Yeagley said. "Working with him and helping him develop over a short period of time made me a better coach. What it took to start from scratch with a player, integrating him in with guys who had played all their lives and trying to find the chemistry and the right roles, those were valuable experiences that I know today were very important in my foundation as a coach. I don't think I would have been nearly as successful if I hadn't had those ten years in club."

1963–1972: The Seasons

The ten years of club play sparked a lot of memories, from playing on slanted fields with poor lighting to trusting a player who had never played in goal before to be your number one goalkeeper. It was all about experimenting, trusting in your teammates, and having fun. "The antics on the field were amusing with entertainment in the backfield," Jeff Richardson said. "We all worked hard and took it seriously, but had a lot of fun. The people on the teams had great personalities and were fun to be around. There was real appeal."

In 1963, Yeagley's first year as head coach, the club team played in ten matches and tallied a 6-1-3 record. They managed to score twenty-seven goals, but they allowed twenty-two. It was a learning season, and the young team took those lessons to heart.

Things improved in 1964. IU posted an 8-1-1 record and tallied forty-three goals, while allowing twenty-three. Little by little, the team was moving in the right direction. The next five years would bring many more wins, as the Hoosiers out-

scored their opponents on their way to a record of 38-14-3, recording 188 goals and allowing 89. The Hoosiers were showing early signs of becoming a dominating force. Then came 1970. That year marked Yeagley's only losing season in his forty-one years at IU. His club team scraped together a 3-8 record. They struggled on both offense and defense, scoring just 14 goals and allowing 33. It wasn't a good sign for a team on a quest for varsity status.

In 1971, a number of newcomers joined the squad, and the new team found a way to make magic. They dominated opponents on their way to a record of 12-0, while outscoring opponents 60 to 6. It was the only undefeated season in Yeagley's years at IU. The coach's faith in his club team was renewed. "Coach Yeagley had his first losing season and was moving backwards," Gary Fresen said. "He didn't have anybody coming back. He was very unsure of what was going to happen. Then my cast of characters showed up, and it

was like a breath of fresh air. We came in and made a difference at a moment in time when it was important to do so. We had an undefeated season and erased the miserable season off the face of the Earth."

The magic continued in 1972, when IU put together an 11-1 record. The team's only loss was a close one, to Eastern Illinois by a score of 3-2. The Hoosiers received an invitation to the NCAA Tournament that year, but they were unable to attend. The administration had signed a letter of intent, thinking that IU would never get invited. When the invitation came and the team asked for support, they were turned down. "Coach Yeagley handled it in a very classy way," Fresen recalled. "A lot of players didn't take it so well."

After ten years under Yeagley, the Hoosiers were receiving national recognition for their successes. They had compiled a record of 78-25-7, recording 379 goals to their opponents' 185. The talent on the field was apparent; despite being only a

Umit Kesim challenges a player during the 1964 season. A true team leader, Kesim was named an All-American, despite the team's club status. Photo: *Arbutus* Archives, 1965.

club team, the Hoosiers had produced three All-Americans. Umit Kesim was the first, in 1966; he was followed by Karl Schmidt in 1967 and Bob Nelson in 1972. The only question was whether the administration would allow a new varsity team. After having their dream of going to the NCAA Tournament taken away, attaining varsity status was now more important than ever.

IU's Fred Norris prepares to take a kick against Illinois in 1964. Jack Jensen awaits the kick and prepares to get the rebound. The Hoosiers won the game 9-1. Photo: *Arbutus* Archives, 1965.

The Quest for Varsity Status

In ten years, the club team had proved itself on the field under Yeagley. The Hoosiers had received national praise. Now

be and steadily planning out what it would take for people to take the team seriously.

"Jerry couldn't have done it by himself," Marilyn Yeagley said. "It was definitely a group effort. He had to get students behind it. There was definitely a movement. And the movement was being charged by Jeff Richardson. He knew which buttons to push. With Jerry being on the faculty, it was almost as though he couldn't initiate it. It had to come from a different source."

Perhaps it was good timing. In the early '70s, students all over America were making their opinions known. There was an

they had a new mission. If they could gain varsity status, they would be allowed to attend the NCAA Tournament and would have full support from the athletic department. They were on an exciting new road, but it wouldn't be a smooth one. Jeff Richardson, student body president at the time, began pushing for varsity status. He used his sources to get in the right doors. He began meeting with the powers-that-

active student movement on every college campus. "If students weren't upset about what war was going on, they were upset about what courses were being taught or what courses weren't being taught, the sexual revolution," Marilyn said. "You name it, there was always something happening on campus. There were signs out and college students boycotting this and getting up in arms about something else.

It was a very, very exciting time, troubling at times. College students at that time were making themselves known."

Richardson knew that the timing was perfect, and he did what he could to make things happen. "When I became student body president, I made a promise to Jerry," he said. "Coach Yeagley already had a great reputation as a club coach. He had a vision that he was going to take IU to great heights in the soccer community and do it with varsity status. I was in a position now to help, and I was also automatically a member of the IU athletic committee. I wanted to use my platform to help the club team gain varsity status."

Richardson teamed up with club captain Gary Fresen and friend of the program Nick Matavuli. The trio vowed to make things happen. "We needed to show the team was a team and wanted it," Fresen said. "Being in political science, I stepped forward to help Jeff. When Coach Yeagley or Jeff needed a meeting, I would go to them. I was sort of the spokesperson. I remember meeting with Herman B Wells. He laid out what our strategy and tactics should be, what my role should be, and what I should tell

those guys." Matavuli volunteered to work on publicity for the campaign. "Nick would cut things out of the newspapers and paste them into posters," Yeagley remembered. "On game days, he would take reserve players out a couple hours before the games. He'd drive his car around campus, and they'd announce the games through megaphones. He was the kind of guy who wouldn't take no for an answer."

Richardson and Fresen met with numerous people. They wanted to publicize what they were up to and rally support. Yeagley stayed out of it. If he got too involved, his job could be in jeopardy. Everyone seemed excited and supportive about the quest at hand, with one exception. Athletic Director Bill Orwig had other plans. He wanted to build a nine-thousand-seat hockey stadium and make hockey the next varsity sport. There hadn't been a new varsity sport in twenty-five years. And if soccer became a sport, hockey wouldn't have a chance.

"I went to Orwig and told him my plan," Richardson said. "He said, with his finger pointing at me, 'Jeff, as long as I am athletic director at Indiana University, soccer will never become a varsity sport.'

Coach Yeagley takes some time to joke with his players during the 1971 season. Photo: *Arbutus* Archives, 1972.

At the 2003 NCAA Championship, Gary Fresen and Jeff Richardson hold up a flag that was at IU's first NCAA Championship appearance in 1976, courtesy of the Koontz family. Fresen and Richardson were instrumental in helping the club team gain varsity status. Photo: Yeagley collection.

I said, 'Thank you for letting me know where you stand. You told me you're not going to support it, but it's going to happen.' He was very unhappy. I was more determined than ever. I was disappointed, but I knew we were going to get varsity status. He made his position clear, and so did I."

The students were actively behind the soccer team. Articles and letters to the editor were printed in the newspapers. An informal committee, led by Richardson, met behind closed doors, often in the Yeagleys' basement. Marilyn Yeagley typed out whatever they needed. It was a well-orchestrated campaign with a ton of supporters. "I never thought we were spinning our wheels, but if it hadn't gone anywhere, it certainly would have been spinning our wheels," Marilyn said. "With the type of personality Jeff Richardson has, when his mind gets set on something, and he knows that it's the right decision, there is no holding back. He knew what he wanted as the end result, and nothing was going to stop him from getting from point A to point B. And Jerry, too, he was so determined to see it become varsity. He saw the direction that soccer was going. No one else saw it in the Midwest. He was blessed with people, players that felt the same way he did and made it all happen."

When judgment day arrived, everyone was a little nervous. But deep down, they believed that they would win the vote.

Richardson had been told before the board of trustees meeting that the vote was in their favor. "I knew when I got there what was going to happen," Richardson said. "The only thing that was going to be interesting would be what Orwig would say. Not one negative thing was said. Then it was Orwig's chance to speak. He said, 'I've long been a supporter of the IU soccer club becoming a varsity sport.' I was very happy that he saw the light and got on board. It was quite a dramatic turnaround from the fall before."

The vote was taken and the decision made: The soccer club was granted varsity status. As of fall 1973, the team would be a full-fledged part of the athletic department. Richardson, the Yeagleys, and all the helpers heaved a sigh of relief. Everything they had worked for was now reality. "When it happened, people were embracing each other," Richardson said. "It was like a wedding. We knew it was going to happen. We were walking down the aisle. But when it did happen, there was a burst of emotion. It was amazing."

A Smooth Transition

The IU athletic department welcomed the soccer program with open arms. The team would now be based out of Assembly Hall, and they would practice on the football practice fields. Their home games would be played at two locations: Memorial Stadium for weekend games, or the Astroturf field with lights up the hill and east of Fee Lane. Their doubleheaders would now be played after football games instead of rugby games. They would have access to trainers and training equipment. And their uniforms would be new. This was the real deal. "We had a pretty nice situation for us," Don Rawson said. "We thought it was great. We had a training room upstairs and a trainer. We thought it was pretty darn nice. We trained and played our games on Astroturf for the most part."

The first time they met in the fall of 1973, Coach Yeagley asked them all to go to the south lobby of Assembly Hall. He told them to wait there and they would all venture down to the meeting room together. "I remember Coach said, 'I want you to stay very, very close, because this is an enormous building with caverns and you can get lost,'" Rawson said. "Wouldn't you know it, the very first doors he went to were locked, so now even he didn't know where to go. We ended up having search parties. It took about twenty minutes before we got everybody back together again in the same place to meet because we all got lost."

Things would be different; that was a given. But when the club turned varsity, there were some things that did not change. On the field the team had operated like a varsity squad from the beginning. Yeagley made sure to keep things the same. "I don't feel there was a big difference between the club and varsity days," Fresen said. "There was no moment of 'Wow, we've really stepped up a notch.' We changed locations. Rather than changing in the HPER or the dorms, we changed in locker rooms. We still trained the same."

The team needed support and publicity now more than ever. "Soccer, because of its uniqueness, was relatively new and had to struggle to build the base," said Dave Martin, former director of the Varsity Club. "Then having someone like Jerry and the people around him there to build that base was great. They put the sheets out on campus and spoke to any dorm, fraternity, or sorority that would listen to them. They really worked at it."

The players enjoyed that aspect of it. They developed relationships with their fans. "My fonder memories as a player were often off the field, getting people in the stands to come watch us play," Rawson said. "You had an obligation that was part of the deal, and that was driven from him. That wasn't to me like a chore. That

The last club team photo, taken in 1972. Some of these players would be playing on a varsity squad less than one year later. Photo: Gary Fresen collection.

was an exciting part of it. How many people could we get to come out and watch us play? Because of that, more people watched us, which led the *IDS* to put more articles in the paper, which allowed us to be recognized on campus. There were a lot of positives from it."

The fans respected their enthusiasm. Besides, Memorial Stadium was a big place. Even with a thousand people in the stands, it seemed empty and somewhat awkward, and the fans looked tiny. But the spectators could sit wherever they wanted, and there were none of the strict rules that were in force at football games there. The fans had the run of the stadium.

The Friday night games were often a big event. Those were generally played on the Astroturf field. "Soccer in those days

was where you went to be seen," Chuck Crabb said. "It was a very social setting where the young men and women came to be seen on a Friday night. We played a lot of Friday night matches on that field. And to this day, the adidas Classic, played Labor Day weekend, draws some of our best crowds. And invariably you see the young men and young women all dressed up to be seen and see who is there. It's a great drawing card for IU students."

With everyone working together, the IU soccer family had turned their dream into reality. Now that the team had gained varsity status, they had everything they needed to build on their success and take it to the next level—winning a national championship.

A New Varsity Sport Emerges

Soccer? In Indiana? You can't be serious. But Jerry Yeagley couldn't have been more serious. He had stuck in there for ten years while others told him that IU soccer would never be granted varsity status. And once that status was granted, the winning began. The team began its first varsity season in the fall of 1973. With the start of a varsity squad, new questions arose: Could this team compete at the varsity level? And would they make it to the NCAA Tournament? Only time would tell.

1973: Starting from Scratch

The Hoosiers had posted a winning overall record in their club days, but with the start of varsity competition, all the old re-

The first-ever varsity team photo, from 1973. Photo: Gary Fresen collection.

cords were erased. The team was starting over from scratch. The Hoosiers wasted no time getting back on the winning track, especially since some of the former club players were now representing the new varsity squad. They knew how to be successful, and they carried that attitude over into varsity play. They blended with the new players to come together for one cause—to make a name for themselves among the best teams in the country. "A lot of the guys on the team were carried over from the club years," Scott Rosen said. "They got to experience the prize. We had a pretty diverse group. We had players from Africa and from all over America. We had a diverse background, but we were a pretty tight group."

The Hoosiers' first varsity match was on the road at Notre Dame, and they made quite an impression. Ibrahima Fall scored the first varsity goal for IU, giving the Hoosiers a 1-0 lead. Steve Burks then added two goals. The defense held Notre Dame to a single goal. IU left South Bend with a convincing 5-1 victory. The Hoosiers then returned to Bloomington to play Goshen at their new home, Memorial Stadium. Indiana wasted no time showing who was in charge. The team dominated the entire match, outshooting Goshen 27-3. Bob Nelson played with a broken arm in a splint, but he still led the Hoosiers' offensive attack, tallying a hat trick. Steve Burks collected his second consecutive two-goal game. The Hoosiers again allowed just one goal en route to a 7-1 victory.

The winning didn't stop there. A 3-1 victory over Wabash was followed by a 5-0 win over Kentucky—the Hoosiers' first varsity shutout, and the first of many to come. Ball State fell next, 2-0, and Burks then led the Hoosiers in a 10-0 rout of Indiana State, scoring a record six goals in one match. IU dominated that game, posting fifty-two shots to ISU's three.

In the first match of a four-game road trip, IU traveled to Cincinnati and posted another victory, 8-2. Two more shutouts followed. The Hoosiers then traveled to Eastern Illinois, and there the hot streak came to an end, as Eastern Illinois scored the lone goal of the match, winning 1-0. It was the Hoosiers' first varsity loss. Nevertheless, they were sitting pretty with a 9-1 record—not a bad start for a first-year varsity squad! In the last four games of the season, Indiana posted three more shutouts and one more loss, 1-0 to Cleveland State. In those three shutouts, the Hoosiers outscored their opponents 18-0.

The Hoosiers ended the 1973 season with a 12-2 record. They were not invited to play in the NCAA Tournament that year, but they had more than proved themselves in their first varsity season, outscoring their opponents 68-7. Goalkeeper Leo Ley ended the season with eight shutouts in fourteen games. Overall, the transition from club to varsity play had been a smooth one. "The experience really didn't change," Don Rawson said. "Coach's approach to winning, his approach to just about everything, didn't change significantly except we were a little higher profile on the radar screen. We still got great coverage in the *Indiana Daily Student*. We used to have games that had tremendous crowds." Added Gary Fresen, "It was classy on the club and classy on varsity. We had the same kind of player, but the teams got better." The 1973 season marked a stellar start for a young program. The next year they would work toward making the NCAA Tournament.

1974: Earning a Trip to NCAAs

The Hoosiers were back and ready for action in 1974. Before the start of the regular season, IU hosted the University of Mexico for an exhibition game. The two teams dazzled the estimated eight thousand spectators with a hard-fought match. At the end of the ninety minutes, the Hoosiers came away with the 1-0 victory, courtesy of a goal by Steve Burks. "It was a great game, very exciting," Tom Redmond said. "It was an electrifying atmosphere. We didn't know what to expect. We thought a team from Mexico would kill us, but we played really well."

The Hoosiers picked up right where they had left off in 1973, starting the season on a winning note. They opened up play by welcoming Notre Dame to their home field. IU easily dominated the contest, posting an 11-1 victory and setting a team record for the most goals scored in a match. Steve Burks returned to his scoring ways, tallying two goals on the evening, along with John Schulenburg and Tim McGonagle.

The Hoosiers then put together a pair of shutouts over Dayton (7-0) and Goshen (2-0) before competing in their first tournament. A number of players stepped up in their first three matches, and IU outscored its opponents 20-1. Junior college transfer Tom Redmond led the way against Dayton, tallying two goals and an assist in a 7-0 rout.

IU hosted the first-ever Indiana State Tournament that year and then proceeded to win it, defeating Purdue 7-1 and Ball State 3-0. With a record of 5-0 so far for the season, the Hoosiers would continue their winning streak. IU won the next five games, posting three shutouts and allowing opposing teams to tally just two goals. In their second year of varsity play, it seemed that there was only one word to describe the Hoosiers' play—domination.

And then came Eastern Illinois. In 1973, the Panthers had shut out the Hoosiers 1-0. This time IU would tally a goal, but it wouldn't be enough, and Eastern Illinois won the game 2-1. It was the Hoosiers' first loss on their home field in their two years of varsity competition. But

the squad rebounded quickly, traveling north to Chicago for the University of Illinois-Chicago Tournament, where they picked up their second tournament title of the year, beating MacMurray 4-1 and Illinois-Chicago 2-1. With a 12-1 record, the Hoosiers had one thing on their minds: making it into the NCAA Tournament.

The Hoosiers had three more games to

Coach Yeagley paces the sidelines during the 1975 campaign. Photo: IU Archives.

showcase their talents before the NCAA would make its selection of teams for the tournament. In the first game, IU welcomed Cleveland State and fell 2-1. It wasn't a good start. But once the Hoosiers lost that game, they vowed not to lose another. They shut out their next two opponents, Earlham 5-0 and powerhouse Michigan State 3-0.

The NCAA Tournament Committee finally took notice. The Hoosiers received their long-awaited invitation to the tournament and looked forward to round-one action. IU traveled to third-ranked SIU-Edwardsville for the team's first-ever NCAA Tournament game. The Cougars tallied two goals in the first half. The Hoosiers fought back, but it wasn't enough. SIU-Edwardsville held on for the shutout, handing IU its third loss of the season. "We ended up losing 2-0 on a very windy, cold, really kind of a nasty day," Redmond said. "I remember whoever was going with the wind, the goalkeeper could punt the ball almost the length of the field. Everyone wondered who's this Indiana team and how did they get in. We had a good showing."

The Hoosiers had made it their goal to get into the tournament, and they had done it. The next step would be winning a couple of games and playing for the championship.

1975: Frustration Sets In

The 1975 season marked a new challenge for the Hoosiers as they looked to build on their 1974 successes. They started the season with a three-game road trip. In a match against the Cincinnati Bearcats, Indiana took fifty-seven shots en route to a 5-2 victory. Freshman Charlie Fajkus stepped up for his team in his Hoosier debut, tallying two goals in the game.

The Hoosiers then posted back-to-back shutouts, defeating Wabash 9-0 and Dayton 4-0, before returning home. Once

again, the team was looking tough. Their record was 3-0, and they had already outscored their opponents 18-2. And by this time, the combination of Steve Burks and Fajkus was proving to be lethal. The Hoosiers won their next three matches, posting a 6-2 win over Goshen and then winning the State Tournament in Bloomington with shutouts over Purdue, 3-0, and Ball State, 4-0.

The Hoosiers then headed out on another road trip, traveling to Akron, where they dropped their first match of the season, 2-1. Again, however, the team rebounded quickly. IU defeated Western Illinois 2-1 the next day. The Hoosiers then traveled to "Soccer City, USA," St. Louis, to play the feisty Billikens in the first meeting for the two teams since IU had gained varsity status. St. Louis put on a show, and the Hoosiers struggled in a 4-1 loss. It was their worst loss in three seasons.

Once again, the Hoosiers returned home and bounced back with a vengeance. In their next three games, they outplayed their opponents, recording three shutouts. IU first handed DePauw a 9-0 loss. The Hoosiers then participated in their first Big Ten Classic, shutting out Wisconsin 5-0 and Michigan State 6-0. Their next match was against Eastern Illinois. The two teams battled into overtime, but to no avail. The game ended in a 1-1 draw—the first tie in IU varsity history.

The Hoosiers played their remaining four matches at home, posting a 3-1 record. The first game resulted in a victory over Illinois-Chicago. But then Cleveland State came to town. The Hoosiers needed this win to improve their chances of making it into the NCAA Tournament. IU dominated play in the second half, but CSU had tallied two goals in first-half action. The Hoosiers attempted to battle back, but they came up one goal short. Cleveland State won the match 2-1, and

Hudson Fortune and Angelo DiBernardo congratulate Charlie Fajkus (*center*) after a game. In Fajkus's four years at IU, he collected thirty-eight goals and thirty-eight assists for 114 points. In his second season, 1976, the Hoosiers made their first Final Four appearance. Photo: IU Athletics.

IU saw its postseason hopes crash to the ground. "Cleveland State and Akron were the two top teams we played," Tom Redmond said. "We lost to both and lost our chances to get into the NCAA Tournament. It was really disappointing. Both games we lost by one goal. We easily could have won, but we came up short."

Nevertheless, the Hoosiers continued to showcase their talent. They shut out their next two opponents, defeating Earlham 8-0 and Kentucky 11-0. It was a nice way to end the season, but it wasn't good enough for the Hoosiers—they wanted to keep going. "We got off to a great start," Redmond said. "We expected to win. We approached that game with that attitude. If there were a couple of breaks here or there, we could have come out on top."

The Hoosiers ended their third season of varsity play with a 13-3-1 record, outscoring their opponents 79-15. They had added a few more superstars to the team and were looking to add some more strength to the lineup in the off-season. They would continue the hunt to earn a trip to the NCAA Tournament and see how far they could go.

1976: Making a Trip to the Finals

The Hoosiers kicked off the bicentennial year with a bang, handing the University of Wisconsin-Milwaukee a 6-0 loss in Bloomington. They then fell flat against Western Illinois in a game that ended in a 0-0 draw. Thereafter, however, they would not look back.

The Hoosiers shut out their next three opponents. After back-to-back 6-0 victories over Dayton and Ball State, they faced Indiana State in the State Classic in West Lafayette. IU easily clinched the Classic title, handing ISU a 19-0 shutout. Rudy Glenn and Ray Kean each tallied a hat trick, while Angelo DiBernardo, Jim Mercurio, Tim Walters, and David Shelton tallied two goals apiece. It was the most lopsided victory in IU varsity history.

The win also marked the Hoosiers' fifth consecutive shutout. They now had a 4-0-1 record, and had tallied thirty-seven goals. There was something special about this '76 team. IU defeated Akron in a close match, a 3-2 overtime victory. And then came the biggest match of the year.

On October 10, the Hoosiers welcomed St. Louis to Memorial Stadium. An unstoppable soccer powerhouse, the Billikens had dominated the national tournament and generally had other teams quaking in their boots. On this day, however, IU would find a way to shut them down. The Billikens managed to tally one goal, but Hoosier freshman phenom Angelo DiBernardo got the ball past the keeper five times. Even *Sports Illustrated* took note. The Hoosiers were finally receiving the recognition they deserved. "What a moment in time," Gary Fresen said. "St. Louis finally puts IU back on its

schedule, makes a trip to Bloomington, and Angelo scores five goals. IU beats them 5-1 and makes it into *Sports Illustrated*."

Even newcomers to the game were impressed. "As a professional staff member, my first exposure to Coach Yeagley was on a Sunday afternoon in Memorial Stadium. Indiana vs. St. Louis," Chuck Crabb said. "We were at a point then of still trying to be the breakout team to establish ourselves. That was a day when Angelo DiBernardo scored, I think, all five goals, as we shut out St. Louis 5-0. Angelo gave the performance that is rarely seen by anyone but the supernova athlete, breakaways, shots that were pure poetry in motion in being scored."

The Hoosiers continued their winning ways for the remainder of the season, claiming the Big Ten Classic and the Wheaton Classic. And in their last three regular-season games, they would avenge a loss and collect three shutouts. Cleveland State had erased IU's chances of going to the tournament in 1975, but the Hoosiers found redemption in 1976, handing CSU a 5-0 loss. They then defeated Earlham 13-0 and Kentucky 7-0 before receiving their second bid to the NCAA Tournament.

Because of their impressive 15-0-1 performance in the regular season, the Hoosiers were ranked No. 2 in the nation, and they would play host for two games in tournament action. First up for IU was Akron in the Midwest Regionals. Glenn and Fajkus tallied goals for the Hoosiers in the team's 2-1 victory over the Zips.

IU then welcomed SIU-Edwardsville to Memorial Stadium. It was a cold, icy late November day, and the players couldn't even get traction on the field. At halftime, IU trainer John Schraeder got hold of some football cleats and passed them out to the team. After changing shoes, the Hoosiers took over the match, winning 1-0. "We always joked Schraeder got the win that day," Redmond said. "We went from a team sliding all over to a team that had control. We dominated the second half."

With that win, the Hoosiers advanced to the team's first College Cup. They traveled to Philadelphia to begin their adventure. In semifinal action, the Hoosiers faced Hartwick. DiBernardo would not start the game, and at halftime the score was 0-0. But in the second half, Yeagley would find a way to make magic. He inserted DiBernardo, who tallied two quick goals. It proved to be enough as IU held on for the 2-1 win. "Coach didn't start him against Hartwick in the semi-

finals," George Perry said. "He comes off the bench and scores two goals. Then Coach takes him out, and we basically just hold on for the rest of the game."

The Hoosiers had done it—they were in the final match and would play for the national title. Not only that, but they were facing San Francisco, the defending national champion. The Hoosiers looked at it not as a negative, but as a challenge. But San Francisco became the only team to find the net on that brisk December day, handing the Hoosiers a 1-0 loss. "I believe the average age of the San Francisco players in '76 was somewhere in the mid to high twenties," Perry said. "Ours was somewhere around eighteen and a half or nineteen. At the time there really wasn't a

Hoosier fans flocked to see their team play St. Louis on October 10, 1976. IU prevailed 5-1, courtesy of five goals by Angelo DiBernardo. Photo: IU Archives.

rule about eligibility. We were playing against men, and we didn't do too badly. It was only 1-0. But San Francisco was definitely a stronger team and probably the better team."

Regardless of the outcome, the Hoosiers had had an incredible run in 1976. They had established themselves on the national stage and made it to the final game. They had posted an 18-1-1 record, the best in varsity history. And they had dominated the goals, outscoring their opponents 94-11. After four years, IU men's soccer had arrived. "I think in 1976, the freshman class wanted to make things happen," Angelo DiBernardo said. "We loved the school. We loved Coach. We just wanted to make it happen. We all worked really hard together to begin the process."

1977: SIU-Edwardsville Strikes Back

Even after a great season, a team has to start from square one the next year. In 1977, the Hoosiers were determined to make it back to the national championship game. "We had basically the same group come back," Angelo DiBernardo said. "We had the experience of being to the finals, and it made us that much better. Having said that, every time we stepped on the field, the game was that much harder."

The Hoosiers had created a major buzz in 1976, and top players from across the country were taking note. They wanted to come to IU to be part of something spectacular. Robert Meschbach, one of the top recruits in the nation, arrived in Bloomington hoping to add to the Hoosiers' success. It didn't take long for the team to pick up where they had left off. As soon as the first whistle blew, the Hoosiers began their domination. They opened on the road with a 1-0 victory over UW-Milwaukee. It wasn't a bad start. But when the

team returned home, the fireworks began. IU defeated Wheaton 6-0, led by an Angelo DiBernardo hat trick.

In the next match, Meschbach made a name for himself, tallying two goals in a 9-0 win at Dayton. Tim Walters added two more. One week later, IU faced a rematch of the 1976 final game vs. San Francisco. This time the teams met in Bloomington. Rudy Glenn stepped up for his Hoosiers, tallying IU's lone goal of the match. San Francisco also managed to score one goal as the teams battled into overtime. No one scored in the extra session, and the game ended in a 1-1 draw.

IU then went on a winning frenzy, collecting six victories, all but one by shutout. The defense was on fire. The streak began with a 5-0 victory over Akron. Next was a 1-0 win over Cincinnati before the Hoosiers returned home to host the Big Ten Classic. They won the Classic in convincing fashion, destroying Michigan State 7-0 and Wisconsin 8-1. The final two shutouts came against Eastern Illinois (1-0) and Illinois-Chicago (2-0).

The team's next match was at Cleveland State. The Hoosiers knew it wasn't going to be easy. They were without defender Mike Freitag, who had suffered a knee injury. Up to that point, IU's defense had allowed just three goals in ten games. CSU decided to give the Hoosiers exactly what it had received from them in 1976—a shutout. Cleveland State outplayed the Hoosiers and handed them their only loss of the regular season, 2-0. It was the only time IU had been shut out in 1977, and the loss ended the Hoosiers' regular-season unbeaten streak at twenty-eight.

IU rebounded quickly again as the team returned to Bloomington for a two-game home stand. The Hoosiers defeated Ball State 11-1 and Purdue 7-0. Then, with one regular-season match remaining, they took to the road, traveling to St. Louis. Every time IU and SLU played, the fans were guaranteed a good match. This game was no exception. The two teams battled it out to the end, with DiBernardo scoring the lone goal of the match in a 1-0 Hoosier victory.

Having ended the regular season with a 12-1-1 record, the Hoosiers awaited their fate. As they'd hoped, they received an invitation to the NCAA Tournament. Seeded third, they began their hunt for a title. Unfortunately, they would not play at home, and they would be up against one of their toughest opponents—SIU-Edwardsville. The last time the two teams had met, IU had knocked SIU-E out of the tournament. This time the roles would be reversed. In a four-overtime battle, Glenn and Hudson Fortune tallied goals for IU. SIU-E added a third goal, winning the game 3-2.

Just like that, Indiana's postseason had come to an end. Nevertheless, it had been a successful run for the Hoosiers. They would be back in 1978 and would try once again to reach their ultimate goal.

1978: Back to the Finals

After an early exit the year before, the Hoosiers looked to be tough in 1978. They had the core of the 1977 team returning, and these guys were hungry for a championship. Yeagley came up with a plan, which included the hardest schedule to date for his players. In their first ten matches, all their opponents would be nationally ranked.

UCLA was up first. It was the Bruins' first trip to Bloomington, and they went back to California with a 2-1 loss. The Hoosiers then took a road trip of their own, heading out east, where they picked up three straight wins, defeating Rhode Island 2-0, Connecticut 4-2, and Springfield 4-0. The team destroyed their opposition. In four matches, they outscored their opponents 12-3.

The Hoosiers then returned home to host the Big Red Classic. IU cruised to a victory in the first game, defeating Penn State 2-0. On day two, the Hoosiers faced Hartwick. Again they took control, posting a 4-0 victory. This team seemed ready for anyone! The Hoosiers packed their bags once again, this time heading to the West Coast. They won their first match 1-0 over San Jose State, courtesy of an Angelo DiBernardo goal. The No. 1 Hoosiers then prepared for a battle against the No. 2 team in the country, San Francisco. Charlie Fajkus gave the Hoosiers a one-goal advantage in the first half. San Francisco found a way to tie, but the Hoosiers refused to give up. DiBernardo tallied a goal of his own for IU, putting the Hoosiers up 2-1. IU held on to the lead and won the match.

The Hoosiers then returned to the Midwest, but they still had two games to play against ranked opponents. They posted a 2-1 victory over Akron and shut out St. Louis 2-0. IU's season had begun with ten games against ten ranked opponents. It was a test, and the team had passed it with flying colors, succeeding beyond Coach Yeagley's expectations. The Hoosiers continued their winning ways, taking another Big Ten Classic with 2-0 and 6-0 wins over Ohio State and Wisconsin respectively. By the end of October, they had compiled an impressive 16-0 record. And then Cleveland State came to town. The Vikings always seemed to find a way to spoil the Hoosiers' fun, and they did so again on October 28, handing IU its first loss of the season by a 1-0 score. A few days later, however, IU defeated Ball State 6-2. At that point the Hoosiers had just three regular-season matches remaining, and they won them all, posting a record of 20-1.

They were back in the NCAA Tournament for the third straight year. In their first match, they welcomed Cleveland State back to Bloomington. The last time

Angelo DiBernardo, Rudy Glenn, and Charlie Fajkus (*in back*) celebrate after taking the lead over Cleveland State in the second round of the 1978 NCAA Tournament. IU won the match 3-1 and advanced to the quarterfinals. Photo: IU Archives.

the teams had met, CSU had come out on top. But this time, the Hoosiers weren't about to let the Vikings end their tournament run. DiBernardo tallied two goals and Robert Meschbach tallied one in a 3-1 win.

IU then faced SIU-Edwardsville. One year prior, SIU-E had ended the Hoosiers' run for a national championship. This time, IU would come out on top, advancing with a 2-0 victory. With the win, the Hoosiers were off to the NCAA College Cup in Tampa. Their first match was against Philadelphia Textile, who were undefeated at 17-0. The Hoosiers didn't let that record intimidate them as DiBernardo and Walters both tallied goals in a 2-0 IU win. The Hoosiers would meet San Francisco in the final.

The title game quickly became a case

of déjà vu. The two teams had met in the 1976 championship, with San Francisco winning the game. But in 1978, when the teams had met in the regular season, the Hoosiers had come out on top, 2-1. This game would be up for grabs. The Hoosiers applied pressure from the start, but San Francisco would dominate. The Dons defeated the Hoosiers 2-0, taking the national title.*

In 1978, the Hoosiers had dominated their opponents again, posting a 23-2 record and outscoring the opposition 77-15. They had made it to another championship game. It wasn't their year to win it

---

*The title was later revoked because San Francisco had played in the tournament with an ineligible player. So the 1978 NCAA Tournament officially ended without a champion.

all, but they would be back in 1979 with a vengeance, looking to make another trip to the finals.

1979: An Unbelievable Season

Every season has a theme, and the theme for 1979 quickly became stopping opponents cold in their tracks. If they can't score on you, they can't win. The Hoosiers began 1979 by participating in the University of Wisconsin at Milwaukee Kickoff Classic. They first defeated UW-Green Bay 5-0, then took the second match from the host team, 2-0. IU's third game ended with a 5-0 shutout over Purdue. Freshman Armando Betancourt led the Hoosiers against UW-M and Purdue, tallying two goals in each match.

IU hosted the 1979 Big Red Classic, welcoming Southern Methodist in the first game. The Hoosiers failed to score a goal, and SMU collected a 1-0 win. It would be Indiana's only loss in the regular season. It was also the first time IU had lost to a team other than Cleveland State in four years of regular-season play. The Hoosiers then embarked on an eighteen-game unbeaten streak. In the second game in the Classic, they faced Appalachian State and posted a 3-0 shutout. They went on to shut out their next four opponents. In the third shutout, a 4-0 victory over Notre Dame, Coach Yeagley earned his 100th career victory.

IU traveled to St. Louis with a 9-1 record and eight shutouts. Only one team, SMU, had scored on the Hoosiers up to that point, and that was just one goal. But St. Louis always liked to make things difficult for Indiana. Mike Freitag tallied the first goal for the Hoosiers as the team worked toward a 3-1 finish. St. Louis attempted to stop IU, but managed to get only one goal into the net.

The Hoosiers returned to shutting out opponents. They first handed Cincinnati a 6-0 loss. The team then hosted the Big

Ten Classic, and the domination continued as IU shut out Illinois and Michigan State by identical 5-0 scores. The next game, against Eastern Illinois, would slow the Hoosiers down. The two teams battled into overtime, but the game ended in a 1-1 draw. The Hoosiers then added two more shutouts to their record, posting 1-0 victories over South Carolina and Evansville.

Next up was Cleveland State, a team that always liked to bring IU's winning streaks to an end. But on this day the Vikings could manage only a single goal. Unfortunately, the Hoosiers could do no better, and they walked away with another 1-1 draw. They then took it upon themselves to sweep the four remaining games, and not allow any more goals. They outscored their opponents 30-0 during that stretch. In the final game of the regular season, IU handed Minnesota a 6-0 loss, winning the Big Ten title match.

The No. 1 Hoosiers then looked to the NCAA Tournament. First up, they would welcome Cleveland State to Bloomington. In contrast to the usual close matches between these two teams, IU dominated the game. Rudy Glenn and Pat McGauley each tallied two goals en route to a 5-0 victory. After posting eighteen shutouts, the Hoosiers faced Penn State. The Nittany Lions gave them a taste of their own medicine, handing the team a 2-0 loss. After setting records and destroying opponents in 1979, the No. 1 team in the nation had been eliminated from the tournament.

The Hoosiers were stunned. "We had all the ingredients, but were a little unlucky," McGauley said. "We set all the records for shutouts, wins. We always expected good things. When we went to Penn State, we should have won. It was a hard game. It was snowing. We weren't in our confines, and we were upset. It was devastating." Betancourt agreed: "We were a pretty dominating team physically in every sense. We were going to win the championship. It was more of a disappointment not winning, because everybody expected us to win."

The team would regroup and get ready to start a new decade. IU wrapped up the 1970s having played just seven varsity seasons. In those seasons, the Hoosiers had dominated opponents and truly become a force to be reckoned with, posting a 111-15-5 record. IU most definitely had arrived.

1980: Almost, but Not Quite

The 1979 season had ended in disappointment for the Hoosiers, and the 1980 season looked to be a rough one as well. IU had graduated eight senior starters and had some huge holes to fill. The Hoosiers were fortunate in having two strong offensive players in Armando Betancourt and Robert Meschbach. But could those two players take the team to the level where it needed to be? No one could predict that, but the Hoosiers had confidence in their coach. "The chemistry was excellent in 1980," Pat McGauley said. "Here was a team that had just lost eight seniors. We certainly wouldn't do well. But Coach has this ability to keep players in the corridor and bring them in when needed."

The team got off to a rocky start. The Hoosiers traveled to Dallas to open up play and fell short of expectations, tying SMU 1-1 and then falling to North Texas State 1-0. They then returned home to face one of the toughest teams in the na-

Pat McGauley tallied twenty-two goals and seventeen assists in his first two seasons as a Hoosier. He ended his career at IU with forty-six total goals and thirty-two assists for 124 points. Photo: IU Athletics.

tion, Connecticut. Betancourt stepped up for IU and tallied an early goal. The Hoosiers held on to the 1-0 lead and took the victory. Betancourt would lead IU again four days later when the Hoosiers traveled to Purdue. He tallied four goals in IU's 10-0 win over the Boilermakers.

The Hoosiers then faced Penn State, the team that had knocked them out of the 1979 tournament. There may have been some new faces among IU's starting eleven, but the Hoosiers still had a bad taste in their mouths from the prior season. They easily took the match, sending the Nittany Lions home with a 2-0 loss.

IU won its next five matches before getting a reality check. With an 8-1-1 record, the Hoosiers faced St. Louis. The Billikens decided that it was time to put an end to IU's winning ways. They outplayed and outscored the Hoosiers on their way to a 3-0 win.

But as with past Hoosier teams, that loss would send IU on a winning frenzy. The Hoosiers kicked things off with a 9-0 slaughter of Cincinnati. Meschbach led IU against the Bearcats, tallying five goals. IU then collected back-to-back shutouts in the Big Ten Classic, posting wins over Michigan State (5-0) and Ohio State (2-0). The shutouts continued as the Hoosiers added three more. No team had scored on IU in six matches. This was definitely a team on a mission! Ball State put an end to IU's shutout streak, managing to tally one goal, but the Hoosiers responded with four of their own to defeat the Cardinals 4-1. Three days later, IU faced Evansville. The Aces also avoided a shutout, tallying two goals. But IU tallied three and won the match 3-2.

The Hoosiers had three matches to play in the regular season, and they continued to dominate, posting three shutouts. In the final game, IU won the Big Ten title with a 2-0 victory over the Wisconsin Badgers. The Hoosiers had posted a 24-0 record against Big Ten opponents.

In NCAA Tournament play, the Hoosiers cruised through their first two matches, shutting out Cleveland State 3-0 and beating Penn State 3-1 en route to the College Cup. They arrived in Tampa for their third Final Four in five years. IU was impressive in semifinal play, posting a 5-0 win over Hartwick.

And then came the moment the team had been waiting for—a chance to win the NCAA Championship. IU would face San Francisco in the final game. The Hoosiers had never won a postseason contest against USF, and 1980 proved to be no different as they fell 4-3. IU had dominated the match, outshooting the Dons 24-9, but the Hoosiers had failed to get the game winner. "We lose a heartbreaker to a team on two crummy goals," McGauley said. "We were up 2-0. They tied it 2-2. Then we were down 2-3. We came back and tied it 3-3. Then they scored a crummy goal in overtime and won. Here we were thinking Coach has lost to the same team three times in the finals. We wondered when we were going to deliver a championship for this guy. He never showed disappointment in the team. It just made him a lot more hungry."

In eight years of varsity play, the Hoosiers had proved that they could tangle with the best of them. But the one goal they had yet to reach was a national championship title. They had had three chances, but had fallen short in each contest. The team vowed to put an end to that. "We knew we had something special at the start," Scott Rosen said. "We usually won games, but the program became more and more national. After '76, people really started taking us seriously. By the late '70s, early '80s, it was natural that IU was going to go to the tournament and the Final Four."

The North stands of Bill Armstrong
Stadium during construction of the
new press box. The original press
box, about half the size of the new
one, is in the middle of the stands.
Photo: IU Athletics.

If You Build It, They Will Come

It had been a frustrating five years for the Indiana soccer program. The team had made three College Cup appearances between 1976 and 1980, but had not been able to get the big win. The Hoosiers needed a breath of fresh air, a new beginning. And in 1981, they got it. The team opened the season in their new home, Bill Armstrong Stadium. The stadium itself had been built for multiple purposes, but the grass field in the center had one primary purpose—to provide a home for the men's soccer team.

Hoosier soccer had had a number of homes in its first few years as a varsity sport—Jordan Field, Memorial Stadium, 10th Street Stadium, the Track Stadium, Woodlawn Field, and a handful of other fields scattered around campus—but each field the team had played on had been shared with someone else. When it came time for the IU Foundation to construct a home for the Little 500 bike race, Bill Armstrong convinced them to put a soccer field in the center.

"When Bill Armstrong Stadium was first established, soccer was a part of it," Don Rawson said. "It was obviously about a bike race and fundraising and another element for the university, but soccer was a part of it. That was a major jump. To have your own fields to train on and your own big-time soccer facility was unbelievable."

Soccer Feet. Photo: Mic Smith, 1989 *Arbutus*.

BILL ARMSTRONG—A SPECIAL FRIEND TO IU SOCCER

When Jerry Yeagley began his quest for varsity status for the soccer team, there were many people who opposed his plan. Among the few who encouraged him to go for it was William S. "Bill" Armstrong, Director of the IU Foundation. Armstrong liked what he was seeing and encouraged Yeagley to always have faith.

"Bill Armstrong took me under his wing and was very supportive," Yeagley said. "He's sort of been the guardian angel of our soccer program from the time he helped us gain varsity status."

Armstrong supported Yeagley and the program until he passed away in 1998. That year the players wore commemorative patches on their jerseys that read "ARMY," in memory of the man who had meant so much to the program. The Hoosiers went on to win the National Championship in '98 and dedicated their win to Armstrong. Even though he may not be with the team physically, Armstrong will always be a part of their success. After all, they play in Bill Armstrong Stadium.

"I think it's fitting for the IU soccer team to play in Armstrong Stadium because Mr. Armstrong was such an important figure in Coach Yeagley's life, in his development as a person, as a coach, as a teacher, as a mentor to all of us," George Perry said. "Every person that Mr. Armstrong met was important to him. He didn't know me that well, but he did know me. I didn't understand why or how he'd know me, but he did."

Bill Armstrong was a special man. He touched many people's lives, including Marilyn and Jerry Yeagley and everyone connected with the IU soccer program. The namesake of the stadium seems to have been the Hoosiers' good luck charm: the team's home record is 216-24-17 since 1981.

The inaugural game at IU's new soccer stadium brought fans out in large numbers. The Hoosiers defeated San Francisco 2-1 in an overtime thriller. Photo: IU Athletics.

A two-story press box was added to the grandstand in 1982. It replaced the temporary box that was built in 1981, during the rush to get the stadium done for the Little 500 and soccer season. Photo: IU Athletics.

Bill Armstrong was known for his work with the IU Foundation. To the IU Soccer family he was a mentor, a friend, and the team's No. 1 fan.

1981: Welcome Home

When Bill Armstrong Stadium, then called the Soccer/Little 500 Stadium, opened its doors to soccer fans, no one was sure how many people would show. But at the opening game of the 1981 season, the stands were filled to capacity. The crowd was there to watch the Hoosiers take on archrival San Francisco, who had beaten IU in the NCAA title match the year before. "That first game, the stadium was absolutely full on the bleacher side, and they were all over the hill," Don Rawson said. "The crowd was estimated at ten thousand. I don't think it was that high, I think it was more like nine thousand, but it was absolutely packed. It was a beautiful day. It was a great atmosphere."

The Hoosiers refused to disappoint their thousands of fans, handing San Francisco a 2-1 overtime loss. Armando

Betancourt and Pat McGauley tallied the two goals for IU. The win marked the second time in Hoosier history that IU had defeated San Francisco. "We waited six months to play the team we lost to in the NCAAs," Pat McGauley said. "And we beat them. It gave us some reward, but it didn't make up for not getting a ring. My claim to fame is that I scored the first goal at Armstrong Stadium. Armando assisted. Then he scored and I assisted. I can still hear the fans pounding on the bleachers. It was such a great day."

Betancourt also recalled the day fondly. "I remember the construction of the new stadium," Betancourt said. "Everybody was anxious to see what it was like. It turned out really nice. The inaugural game we played against San Francisco. We ended up winning 2-1. I scored the second goal. But regardless of who scored the goals, it was a good inauguration. The stands were packed. It was the beginning of a new era."

The Hoosiers began the season with a 2-1 record on the road. Playing in their new home was the start of good things to come for the squad. They did not lose a regular-season game at Armstrong Stadium for the remainder of the year, en route to an 11-0 home record. Their remaining road record was almost as impressive: they lost just one more match in regular-season play, a 1-0 decision to St. Louis on the Billikens' home turf. After that loss, IU strung together a thirteen-game winning streak. A 6-1 win against Louisville at home was followed by a 7-1 win over Southern Indiana and an 8-0 decimation of Illinois. The team was once again on fire.

The Hoosiers endured a close call when they traveled up north to face the University of Wisconsin at Milwaukee. The two teams battled in a close match, with Joe Schmid tallying the lone goal of the game at the end of the first half. The Hoosiers continued their winning ways, posting eleven shutouts on the season, seven in their last eight games. Ball State was the only team to score on IU in the final stretch when the teams met in Bloomington on October 28. But one goal would be it for the Cardinals, as IU got the 7-1 win.

IU entered NCAA action with a 19-2 record, welcoming Wisconsin to Armstrong Stadium for round-one action. The teams had played just two weeks prior, as IU had closed out its regular season by handing the Badgers a 1-0 loss and winning the Big Ten title. Wisconsin returned to Bloomington ready for action, but it was IU that would come out and take charge. Betancourt and Dave Boncek tallied two goals apiece as the Hoosiers cruised to a 5-1 victory.

The Hoosiers moved on to face Philadelphia Textile in quarterfinal action. They dropped a 1-0 decision, then saw their Final Four hopes crash to the ground. "We were dominated the first half," Paul DiBernardo said. "They had the home field advantage and the home crowd. We came out hesitant. We weren't playing well. I remember at halftime Coach said, 'You guys need to get your act together and figure things out.' We got fired up second half and outplayed them. But we weren't able to win the game."

By season's end, opponents had learned to fear the lethal combination of McGauley and Betancourt. Betancourt celebrated his final season as a Hoosier by winning the Hermann Trophy. He tallied twenty-seven goals and sixty-three points for the season. McGauley, who had tallied forty points on the season, would be back for more. "We never expected to lose," McGauley said. "We went into seasons, games, championships expecting we were going to win. We wanted to get a championship with Armando, one of the best players Coach would ever have. We were unfortunate to not score some goals."

IU finished the 1981 season with a 20-3 record. The team had lit up opponents' nets, for a total of eighty-three goals, and the defense had stood strong in the back, allowing just fifteen goals. Everything had seemed to be in place for the Hoosiers, but the last goal failed to go into the net, and another season came to a disappointing end.

1982: NCAA Champs, Finally

Magic. Destiny. Call it what you will, the 1982 season would defy all the odds. The Hoosiers had lost some great talent following 1981. Not only that, but Pat McGauley would be sidelined with a broken leg. But champions don't make excuses; they get the job done. The early part of the season did not go as planned. The Hoosiers lost three of their first four games, all in overtime. They scored eight goals and allowed seven. This wasn't a typical Hoosier squad.

After the third loss, the Hoosiers vowed that there would be no more. And they were right: IU went on a twenty-one-game unbeaten streak. It began with a 4-2 win over Stanford. "In previous years, IU always had one player that was considered a superstar," Paul DiBernardo said. "Maybe at times the team depended too much on those players. In '82, we had to be more of a team because we didn't have that one

The Hoosiers celebrate their first NCAA Championship in 1982. IU defeated Duke 2-1 in eight overtimes. Photo: IU Athletics.

superstar. We started on a bad note, 1-3. After we lost the game against San Francisco, I said we weren't going to lose any more. I felt the team was capable of winning it all."

Certain players took it on as a personal challenge. DiBernardo scored in each of the next seven games. Goalkeeper Chris Peterson and defender Dan "Dipper" King tightened up the back line. In the Hoosiers' next match, they blanked SIU-Edwardsville, 1-0. That would be the first in a string of five straight shutouts. In fact, IU posted ten shutouts in its next eleven games. The Hoosiers stepped up to the task in a big way, outscoring opponents 38-1. During the winning streak, they posted an 8-0 victory over Kentucky and a 7-0 victory over Michigan State. The team was fired up.

In the last game in October, IU battled Evansville down to the wire. The in-state rivals always had intense matches. The Aces not only scored on the Hoosiers but also took them into overtime. The game ended in a 1-1 draw. The Hoosiers then put together two shutouts, 1-0 and 3-0, over Southern Indiana and Dayton respectfully. IU played at Wisconsin for the Big Ten title match. The teams battled into overtime, with IU taking the 2-1 victory.

Going into the NCAA Tournament, the Hoosiers had a 17-3-1 record. They would host the first three matches on their home turf. First up, IU faced Evansville in a do-or-die situation. On a rainy day in Bloomington, the Hoosiers took charge early, gaining a 1-0 advantage. Evansville failed to answer the goal, and IU finally collected a win against the Aces. The Hoosiers then cruised through the next match with a 2-0 victory over Philadelphia Textile, the team that had ended their dreams in 1981. Next up, IU would face SIU-Edwardsville in the semifinals.

Indiana prevailed again, 1-0, and moved on to the finals.

The Hoosiers had been to the finals three times before, in 1976, 1978, and 1980, but this time would be different. IU met Duke in Ft. Lauderdale for the NCAA Championship. Duke was undefeated on the season. The Hoosiers had lost three matches, but their last loss had been twenty games prior. On a hot, humid night in southern Florida, the game was up for grabs. Duke came out with intense speed, and the Hoosiers relied on their strength and skill to try and slow down the Blue Devils. Indiana scored first, but Duke found a way to tie. The teams battled through the end of regulation to a 1-1 draw.

It was a classic standoff. As the teams battled through seven overtime periods, exhaustion took its toll, and players began collapsing as they ran up the field. In the eighth overtime period, Duke was called for a foul just outside the 18. Indiana stepped up to take the freekick opportunity. A handful of Hoosiers positioned themselves around the ball, while Duke made a wall in front of their left goal post.

John Stollmeyer took off and ran around the right end of the wall. A Duke player took a step to his left to try and throw Stollmeyer off. Just as he moved aside, Gregg Thompson took a shot and sent it buzzing past the Duke player's head. It bounced once and went into the net, giving IU the 2-1 victory. The Hoosiers had settled the score at the 159:16 mark. "It was an amazing shot, an amazing play," recalled *Herald-Times* reporter Andy Graham. "You couldn't have asked for a more perfect shot. It was unbelievable."

The players mobbed Thompson and collapsed in a heap of celebration. They then went looking for their coach. The

Hoosiers hoisted Yeagley onto their shoulders and paraded around the field in joy. Finally, they had done it! After only ten years as a varsity team, IU had achieved the ultimate goal—winning the NCAA Championship. "Certainly the first championship got the monkey off our back, after playing in the championship three times," Yeagley said. "Winning in '82 was the special feeling that I'll never forget. Once you win a championship, you want more. You get driven. It's not an end in itself."

And driven the Hoosiers proved to be.

1983: Let's Make It Two in a Row

Everyone was still on a high from winning the '82 championship when they returned to training in the fall of 1983. There was buzz that the team would do it again. But realistically, what were the odds? St. Louis, San Francisco, and Michigan State were the only teams to have captured back-to-back championship titles since 1959. MSU had accomplished that feat once, while the other two soccer powerhouses dominated the record books.

IU started off the season on a sour note, losing 2-1 to Penn State. But that would be it. The Hoosiers then went on a twenty-five-game unbeaten streak, starting with a 2-1 victory over George Mason. Once the winning began, IU never looked back. They weren't all easy, though. The Hoosiers played in nine overtimes that season, four of which ended in ties: Duke 0-0, St. Louis 2-2, Akron 0-0, and Alabama A&M 1-1. Other than those four matches, IU won every game, posting thirteen shutouts. The Hoosiers had two games in which they outscored opponents by double digits, an 11-0 win over Northwestern and a 14-0 win over Louisville. This team could score goals!

IU wrapped up the regular season by winning the Big Ten Eastern Tournament in Columbus with 4-2 and 4-1 wins over Michigan State and Ohio State. The Hoosiers then tied with Alabama A&M before heading to Wisconsin. For the third consecutive year, the Hoosiers and Badgers would face off in the Big Ten title match. This time, IU posted its most convincing win to date, a 4-0 shutout. Indiana would take a record of 17-1-4 into NCAA Tournament action.

IU met Akron in the first game of the tournament. The teams' last meeting had ended in a 0-0 draw. This time, the Hoosiers would get on the board first. But it was Akron that actually scored the goal for IU, accidentally sending the ball into their own net. The Zips then tied the game up, sending it into overtime. Mike Hylla scored the winning goal, and the Hoosiers moved on to the next round. Next up for IU was an old nemesis, St. Louis. The teams battled through the rain, with Iker Zubizerreta and Mark Laxgang each tallying a goal for the Hoosiers in the team's 2-1 win. In the third round, IU faced Virginia. The Hoosiers fell behind 1-0, but they refused to give up. Laxgang netted two goals, while Paul DiBernardo tallied the third, giving IU the 3-1 victory.

The Hoosiers headed back to Ft. Lauderdale to face Columbia in the championship match. The two teams battled it out for ninety minutes, with neither defense allowing a goal. The game went into overtime—nothing new for the Hoosiers, who had played in seven overtimes so far that season, posting a 2-1-4 record in those games. "I remember going into the game they said Columbia was a finesse team while Indiana was more of a physical team," John Stollmeyer said. "We were out there to win a championship. No matter how fancy players are, they still know how to hit."

The Hoosier defense remained solid

against Columbia. IU's Pat McGauley found a way to make up for sitting out during the 1982 championship. Rodrigo Castro passed to McGauley, who sent the ball into the net, giving IU the 1-0 victory. "As fate would have it, the guy that couldn't play in '82 scored in '83," McGauley said. "What bigger joy can you have than scoring the biggest goal of your career in your last game?"

The Hoosiers celebrate their second consecutive NCAA Championship after a 1-0 overtime win over Columbia in 1983. Photo: IU Athletics.

be didn't play as well as we could have. We may not have played the best, but we showed character and made it to the final."

"I couldn't have been happier that we won in 1982," McGauley said. "Every single player on the team said to me, 'Don't worry, Pat, we'll be back there next year.' Those were empty words. To come through was phenomenal. A team made a prom-

The Hoosiers rejoiced again as they became the first team to win back-to-back championships since San Francisco in 1975–76. "Now we're expected to get to the final," Paul DiBernardo said. "We've been there and won it. As a team, we may-

ise to its player that they would win again and it happened."

Yes, it really had happened. IU had captured back-to-back titles. The team would celebrate their latest victory and then look to 1984.

1984: Why Not Go for Three?

They had already won two straight titles, so why not add a third? That's what the 1984 Hoosiers had in mind. The team had lost four starters, but they had no plans to let that stop them. "The team I walked into in 1984 was in the middle of an unbeaten streak," John Trask said. "They had won two national championships in a row. It was just a tremendous group of guys in terms of their character and their quality."

The Hoosiers picked up where they had left off in 1983: winning. They opened the season on the road, traveling to Las Vegas, where they defeated San Diego State 2-1 and UNLV 3-2. They then returned home to host the adidas-MetLife Classic. IU began the tournament against Virginia. The Cavaliers put up a fight from the start, but Indiana's John Stollmeyer would be the one to take charge. He scored a first-half goal that proved to be the only one in the game. The Hoosiers held on for the 1-0 victory.

Indiana then faced Clemson for the first time in school history. The Hoosiers and Tigers battled into overtime, where IU prevailed. The 4-3 victory marked Jerry Yeagley's 200th career win. "We're the team to beat now," Paul DiBernardo said. "We're expected to win. The pressure was on, but we didn't feel it. We were taking it one game at a time."

The Hoosiers won their next four matches before meeting St. Louis at Armstrong Stadium, where the two teams battled to a 2-2 draw. The winning then picked right back up, as IU went on a hot streak, taking ten straight matches. A 4-3 victory over Ohio State sent the Hoosiers on a winning frenzy. Then came Wisconsin. The two teams met in another Big Ten title match. This time the battle would end in a 0-0 draw. The Hoosiers had not yet lost a match in 1984.

IU traveled to the Tampa Classic to wrap up regular-season play. In day-one action, the Hoosiers defeated Tampa 3-1. Two days later, the situation would be reversed as South Florida beat the Hoosiers 4-3. "We lost to South Florida," Paul DiBernardo said. "We deserved to lose that game. We were outplayed. It was sad that we lost. But in retrospect, maybe losing that game was the best thing to happen to us right before the tournament. We had to step it up. Subconsciously we were unstoppable."

The loss snapped IU's forty-six-game unbeaten streak. But the Hoosiers' luck ran out for only that one day, and then it was back to action. IU took a 19-1-2 record into NCAA Tournament play. The Hoosiers received a first-round bye and welcomed Evansville to Armstrong Stadium in round two. IU wasted no time taking control, shutting out the Aces 5-0. "The games against Evansville were always tough, hard-fought games," John Stollmeyer said. "There was nothing easy about those games. The score was generally 1-0. When we beat them 5-0, we let them know we were serious."

IU then welcomed St. Louis back to town. The Hoosiers had a 2-0 lead at halftime, but the Billikens rallied in the second half, scoring twice. Before the final whistle blew, Tim Hylla and Manuel Gorrity had both scored late goals, ensuring that IU would advance with a 4-2 win. In the next round, the Hoosiers hosted Hartwick. The game was intense, and after seventy minutes, the score was tied at 1-1. The Hoosiers needed some magic. Enter Mark Laxgang. On September 23, Laxgang had broken his foot against Notre Dame. Now he was ready to return. Laxgang entered the match at the 67:25 mark. He passed to Hylla, who netted the game-winning goal. IU was headed to its third straight NCAA Championship.

The Hoosiers faced Clemson in the

Mike Hylla (*left*), Iker Zubizerreta, and John Stollmeyer congratulate Paul DiBernardo after he scored the tying goal in the 1984 NCAA Championship game vs. Clemson. Clemson would break the tie and go on to win the championship. Photo: Eric Marshall, 1985 *Arbutus*.

title match at the Seattle Kingdome. The carpet had been shampooed the night before in an attempt to remove the football logos and lines. At game time, the normally dry indoor field was a slippery mess. The teams battled for more than seventy minutes without giving up a goal. Clemson scored at the 78:46 mark. Paul DiBernardo stepped up for IU and tallied a goal five minutes later. But with just 1:42 remaining on the clock, Clemson scored again for a 2-1 lead.

IU put on the pressure, but the Hoosiers failed to score in the remaining minutes of the match. Their luck had run out. The players stood there in disbelief as their three-peat fell short by one goal. "We lost a tearjerker in Seattle at the Kingdome against a team we had beaten earlier in the season," Trask said. "They were a good team, but the surface wasn't right. It was just a strange day. I think everybody felt given a different scenario, we would have won that game. It was a disappointing finish."

The eight players who had brought so much promise to IU as freshmen saw their careers end one win short of a three-peat. "We didn't play as well as we were capable of," Paul DiBernardo said. "That would have been a great way for eight guys to end their career together. But we fell a little short." It was time for the team to reload.

1985: Bring In Some New Guys

With a disappointing finish to the 1984 season, the Hoosiers looked to rebuild in 1985. They kept their standards consistent, wanting to return to the NCAA Championship. It would prove to be a grueling year.

IU started off the season in winning fashion, posting an impressive 5-0 victory over Hartford. But that would be the only win for a while, as the Hoosiers dropped their next four matches. They scored only

two goals in their own adidas-MetLife Classic, falling 3-2 and 1-0 to Clemson and UCLA respectively.

The Hoosiers managed to pick things back up with two straight 4-0 victories over Ohio State and Notre Dame. And the scoring didn't stop there. In the next match, IU posted an 8-1 slaughter of Purdue. In three matches, the Hoosiers had outscored their opponents 16-1. It looked like a new beginning. But the team then dropped another match, to St. Louis, 2-1.

The Hoosiers rebounded, putting together seven straight victories. Their only tie came against Bowling Green, 3-3. After the seven-game streak, IU would welcome Evansville to Armstrong Stadium. The Aces put an end to the Hoosiers' winning ways, handing them a 3-0 loss. IU again rebounded with a 4-0 win over Michigan State. The team then headed to the McDonald's Classic in Ft. Lauderdale, where they ended the season by dropping their last two games of the regular season: to Florida International, 2-1, and to Fresno State, 1-0.

Things were looking a bit bleak for the Hoosiers. Their rebuilding year had fallen short of expectations. In the first round of NCAA Tournament play, IU handed Akron a 2-0 loss. But one week later, the Hoosiers' hopes of advancing to the title game came crashing down. IU traveled to Evansville, to meet the Aces on their home turf. The Hoosiers were looking to avenge their loss from a month earlier and advance to the next round. Evansville, however, had plans of its own. The Aces handed the Hoosiers another 3-0 shutout.

IU finished the season with a 12-9-1 record—the most losses in varsity history. "1985 was a very frustrating year," John Stollmeyer said. "We graduated a lot of seniors, and we brought in a lot of freshmen. At that point in time there was an element among the team that we weren't able to play at the highest level. We didn't have the mental toughness. Three or four of us had it, and that wasn't enough."

1986: Breaking the Streak

The returning Hoosiers knew that the 1985 season had not been representative of Indiana University soccer. They were looking to change things in 1986. Indiana kicked off the new season with a 2-1 loss to South Carolina, then tied Virginia 1-1. When Notre Dame came to town for the third game of the season, the Hoosiers picked things up, prevailing over the Irish by a score of 2-0. They then went on to win their next four games. Michigan State was the only team to score on IU, but the Hoosiers still pulled off the 3-1 victory. The biggest win, a 5-0 victory over Cincinnati, showed that IU was in top form.

The Hoosiers had a 5-1-1 record only seven games into the season. They had outscored their opponents 16 to 4. They were looking tough. They then welcomed St. Louis to Armstrong Stadium. Once again the Billikens found a way to break down the Hoosiers, holding IU to a single goal. St. Louis also found a way through Indiana's defensive line, tallying three goals and handing the Hoosiers their second loss of the season, 3-1.

IU quickly rebounded, beating Miami of Ohio 5-0. The Hoosiers then struggled on the road at Akron, falling 1-0. Five days later, they posted a 3-2 victory against Wisconsin-Green Bay, followed by 2-0 victories against Wisconsin-Milwaukee and Cleveland State. By mid-October, the Hoosiers had a 9-3-1 record. They looked to be on track to make it back to the NCAA Tournament. But then a black cloud moved over the program.

The Hoosiers tallied a 2-2 tie in their next game, against Marquette. They then fell to Clemson 3-1. IU rebounded for 1-1 ties in its next two games against Ameri-

can and Evansville. For the third time in two years, IU had failed to beat the Aces. "Evansville really seemed to have our number," Han Roest said. "I truly felt we were outplayed by a team that had less skill than us. It was a telling sign of our performance."

Those two ties would be Indiana's last sign of hope. The Hoosiers would lose their last two matches of the season, allowing five goals and scoring just two. They ended 1986 with a 9-6-4 record. "In 1986 we had a mediocre team," Ken Godat said. "It was kind of an off team for IU soccer. We were good. We just weren't up to the caliber that the program expected. We lost a bunch of seniors from the year before. It was a rebuilding year."

Indiana had received a wake-up call. The Hoosiers had made their first tournament appearance in only their second year as a varsity team, 1974. After missing the next year, they had then made it to ten straight tournaments. In 1986, they suddenly found themselves excluded from the big dance. They had scored a pathetic thirty-six goals on the season, while allowing twenty-one. It was time to make some changes.

1987: Climbing to the Top

It had been a rough two years for the Hoosier program, but 1987 held the promise of a new beginning. The team had found a solid scorer and a goalkeeper they could rely on. "In 1987 Ken Snow arrived," *Herald-Times* reporter Andy Graham said. "He was a prolific scorer. Arriving at the same time was a goalkeeper named Juergen Sommer who was prolific at the other end of the field. They really pieced together some nice teams."

Often, some new blood is all it takes. The Hoosiers dropped their first game 3-1 to South Carolina. But the next day, against SMU, Ken Snow announced his arrival, scoring twice and leading the Hoosiers to a 2-1 victory. Indiana then destroyed Michigan State 6-0 before suffering a heartbreak overtime 4-3 loss to Notre Dame two days later. But that loss would be it for a while. "Coach Yeagley was distraught because our freshman team was supposed to be so strong," Sommer said. "You could see the fire in his eyes. To let Notre Dame get one over on us, he was not happy. We turned it around from there."

The Hoosiers pulled things together in a big way, collecting sixteen straight wins, including nine shutouts. They kicked off the winning streak with a 3-1 defeat of Memphis State. A number of Hoosiers got on the board in that game. In the next match, five different Hoosiers scored, as IU handed Ohio State a 5-0 loss. It was a special day for senior John Trask, who scored the first goal of his college career.

The winning streak included an 8-0 victory over Miami of Ohio, along with back-to-back 7-0 wins over Northwestern and Marquette. Against Marquette, IU scored twice before halftime, then exploded for five more in the second half. The Hoosiers continued their winning ways up through the last regular-season game. They welcomed Wisconsin to Armstrong Stadium and promptly handed the team a 2-0 loss. In the match, Snow tallied a record-setting twenty-eighth goal. IU celebrated as the team won the Big Ten title. With the win, Indiana's winning streak improved to sixteen. The Hoosiers looked unstoppable. "I felt we had a good chance of winning the championship in 1987," Han Roest said. "After we won sixteen games, I felt we couldn't lose."

With an 18-2 record, IU received an invitation to the NCAA Tournament. The Hoosiers faced Clemson at home in second-round action. The Tigers put on a show and handed Indiana a 2-1 loss.

"Clemson had a really dynamic striker, Bruce Murray," Sommer said. "He was very mature. He scored two great goals on us, and we couldn't recover." IU exited the tournament in the second round, but the team was much improved. The Hoosiers ended the season with an 18-3 record and the top rank in the country. They also got their scoring back on track, outscoring opponents 74-20.

1988: Return to Prominence

In 1987 the Hoosiers had found themselves back in the spotlight. They proved that they hadn't lost their magic touch. And in 1988 they would have a chance to prove it all over again. Ken Snow was returning as the nation's leading scorer, and a defense that had allowed just twenty goals and posted ten shutouts would also return, led by goalkeeper Juergen Sommer. This was a talented team from front to back. Anything was possible in 1988.

The Hoosiers kicked off the new season by winning the adidas-MetLife Classic with 2-0 and 2-1 wins over North Carolina and UCLA respectively. Snow led the way, scoring all four goals of the weekend. The Hoosiers then faced Notre Dame. The teams battled in a grueling overtime, but the final score remained 1-1. Two days later, IU shut out Michigan State 6-0. The winning continued.

The Hoosiers posted four more wins before facing nemesis St. Louis. It didn't take long for them to take charge. Snow collected a hat trick and Sommer a shutout in a 3-0 Hoosier victory. IU then tallied its second 6-0 victory of the year in a win over Miami of Ohio. The Hoosiers next took a trip to the Kenny Kent/Aces Classic in Evansville. It proved to be the lowest point of their season, as they dropped both games, 2-1 to Santa Clara and 1-0 to George Washington.

IU strung together four more wins be-

fore heading back to Evansville, where the Hoosiers fell to the Aces by a 1-0 score. That would be their last loss of the season. The Hoosiers rebounded with a 2-0 win over Wisconsin. The team took to the road for the South Carolina-MetLife Classic, where they collected back-to-back ties to close out the season, 0-0 vs. Stanford and 1-1 vs. South Carolina.

At the end of the regular season, IU sat with a No. 9 ranking and a 15-3-3 record. The Hoosiers would make the tournament, but the team had no idea what their future would hold. After sitting out round-one action, IU welcomed Boston to Bloomington. The Hoosiers easily shut down the Terriers, 3-1. IU then welcomed Seton Hall to town. The Hoosiers prevailed again, with another 3-1 victory.

The Hoosiers then received good news: they would host the 1988 College Cup. With a 17-3-3 record, IU could win a championship. The team had to win two games, but this time they had home field advantage. "At the beginning of the season, we lost three games and didn't dominate," Han Roest said. "The team gelled going into the tournament. All the pieces came together. And it didn't hurt that we were playing at home."

In the first match, IU went up against Portland and a stellar defense. Future Premier League and U.S. National Team goalkeeper Kasey Keller stood solid in goal for the Pilots. Prior to the match with IU, Portland had allowed only six goals. But the Hoosiers found a way to score. IU's Simon Katner tallied a goal at the 43:38 mark. The Hoosiers held on to that 1-0 advantage for the remainder of the game, earning the right to meet Howard in the championship match.

The two teams would battle for a grueling ninety minutes. IU was facing another future Premier League keeper in Shaka Hislop. Only one team could win the title, and the Hoosiers found a way to do it. A Howard player took down Ken Snow in the box. The referee awarded a penalty kick. Sean Shapert stepped up to the line for the Hoosiers and converted the penalty kick. That one goal proved to be enough, and IU took the 1-0 victory. The Hoosiers had won another national championship. And this time they had done it on their own field—Bill Armstrong Stadium.

Ken Godat sat out the 1988 season with a knee injury, but he watched the game from the sidelines and cheered his team to victory. "We didn't play very well Friday night against Portland," Godat said. "Howard played against South Carolina in the other semifinal. Howard put on a clinic. We just didn't have a good game. We won, squeaked into the final. Everybody expected Howard to come out and take it to us. Magic happened. We had a good game. Shapert scored the penalty kick. It was an electric feeling once we scored that PK. With the IU defense, we knew we had it. Everybody stepped up that day."

The crowd gave IU a standing ovation, as the players hoisted their coach skyward. The Hoosiers celebrated alongside their fans, who had braved the brisk December air to cheer their team on to victory. It was a special day at Bill Armstrong Stadium, one that fans would never forget. "Americans complain about 1-0 soccer games," Chuck Crabb said. "I think the best soccer game I ever saw was Indiana beating Howard 1-0 in the '88 NCAA Championship. Recalling Marc Behringer with the most unbelievable defensive performance, shutting down Caribbean natives that were the striking forwards for Howard. And he just chewed them up."

All the championships had been special. But this one was especially sweet because it was won in front of the home crowd. Yeagley and his team vowed to be back in 1989 and defend their title with class.

Tom Casaburo and Matt Isger celebrate IU's NCAA Championship win at Bill Armstrong Stadium in 1988, raising their trophies in appreciation of the home crowd fans. Photo: Mic Smith, 1989 *Arbutus*.

Ken Snow and Steve Snow led the Hoosiers
into the Final Four in 1989. Steve tallied the
lone goal against Howard, advancing the
Hoosiers to their second consecutive Final
Four. Photo: Mic Smith, 1990 *Arbutus*.

A Nine-Year Drought

The Hoosiers had now won the NCAA Tournament three times. They were bringing in some of the top young players in the country. Yet after that third national title, their postseason success seemed to fizzle out. It would be another nine years before they would win another championship.

1989: Back to the Final Four

Coming into the 1988 season, the Hoosiers were on top of the world. "Things were on a high," Chad Deering remembered. "Everybody was excited. We had a good recruiting class my year coming in. We had two national team players. We had such a good team." IU began the season with a 1-0 loss to Virginia in the first game of their own adidas-MetLife Classic. They rebounded the next night with a 1-1 tie vs. St. Louis, then headed west to San Francisco to play in the adidas–MetLife Classic, where they defeated Stanford 1-0 and San Francisco 2-0. In a match against Harvard on September 24, Ken Snow had the best game of his career, recording a hat trick in the first half and adding a fourth goal in the second half. His younger brother, Steve, scored earlier in the match and assisted on two of Ken's goals. Between them, the Snow brothers recorded twelve points in IU's 7-2 win. IU played its last home match of the regular season against Great Lakes

Region rival Evansville. The game heated up fast. Three Evansville players received red cards in the first half, allowing the Hoosiers to cruise to an easy 4-0 victory. The team wrapped up the season at the Southern Bell Classic in Ft. Lauderdale, picking up two victories, 2-1 over George Mason and 7-0 over Florida International.

The Hoosiers had a 16-1-2 record heading into NCAA Tournament play. They received the No. 3 seed and sat out round-one action with a bye. In the second round, they continued their winning streak, holding George Washington scoreless in a 4-0 shutout. In the next round, IU faced nemesis Howard. The two teams had met a year earlier in the NCAA Championship at Bill Armstrong Stadium, with Indiana taking the 1-0 victory. Now they were battling it out again, and once again the Snow brothers stepped up for the Hoosiers. Ken passed to Steve, who netted the lone goal of the match for a 1-0 victory.

In the semifinal match against Santa Clara, Steve Snow was on fire for IU. He gave the Hoosiers a 2-0 lead early in the first half, but the Broncos tied the game before intermission. In the second half, Santa Clara increased the pressure, tallying two more goals and handing IU a 4-2 loss. It was only the fourth time in school history that the Hoosiers had allowed four goals. Their tournament hopes were dashed as they were forced to make an early exit. "In 1989 our team was equally as good as the team that won it in 1988," Ken Godat said. "We had a bad fifteen minutes against Santa Clara. The game was at Rutgers. It was like ten degrees. The field was frozen. It was miserable. If we had played them on a good field, we would have taken them." The Hoosiers ended the season with an 18-2-2 record and outscored their opponents 68-18.

With the close of 1989, the Hoosiers wrapped up a decade of excellence. The team had made the NCAA Tournament every year except for 1986, appearing in six College Cups and winning three NCAA Championships. They ended the 1980s with a 182-35-18 record.

1990: Short of Expectations

The Hoosiers were ranked No. 7 at the start of the 1990 season. With six seniors, including Ken Snow and goalkeeper Juergen Sommer, they looked like the team to beat. But the first two matches of the season showed a different side of the Hoosiers. IU kicked off its season at the UNLV Classic in Las Vegas, dropping two straight matches, 3-0 to UCLA and 2-0 to UNLV. It was a bleak beginning for a team that had exhibited so much promise.

The Hoosiers returned home to Armstrong Stadium for the adidas-MetLife Classic. First up, they faced San Francisco. The teams battled to a 2-2 draw. After three games, IU's record stood at 0-1-2. Next up for the Hoosiers was Virginia. Freshman Mirsad Bubalovic would become the hero of the day. Chad Deering passed to Bubalovic, who finished the shot, breaking a 1-1 tie and giving IU the 2-1 victory. The win gave the Hoosiers the confidence that they needed. They won their next eleven matches before tying Northern Illinois on October 17.

On October 3, the Hoosiers faced Cin-

cinnati. For Hoosier fans, it would be a game to remember. Ken Snow would lead Indiana to a 3-1 victory. The two goals he scored put him at the top of the Hoosiers' record books for goals and points. The game also marked Jerry Yeagley's 300th victory at IU. The Hoosiers did not drop a game against Big Ten opponents that year, increasing their conference unbeaten streak to sixty-six games. They then dropped their last match of the season, 2-1 to South Carolina.

It was NCAA Tourney time again. IU went into the postseason with a 14-3-2 record. The Hoosiers easily defeated the University of Wisconsin-Milwaukee 5-1 in round one. They had a close call in round two, handing St. Louis a 2-1 loss. IU gave up home field advantage and took to the road for the third round, heading south to Evansville to face the Purple Aces. On a windy afternoon, it seemed that nothing could go the Hoosiers' way. Evansville dominated play in the first half, tallying the lone goal of the half at the 22:57 mark. In the second half, IU turned up the offensive pressure, but to no avail. The Aces would hold on for a 1-0 victory, ending IU's run for its third consecutive Final Four.

The Hoosiers fell short of their NCAA Championship expectations in 1990, ending the season with a 16-4-2 record, but they nevertheless raked in the awards. Ken Snow won his second Hermann Trophy, and he was Missouri Athletic Club Player of the Year for the second consecutive year. He ended his IU career as the Hoosiers' leader in goals (84) and points (196). Juergen Sommer picked up the adidas Goalkeeper of the Year award, while Jerry Yeagley became the sixth coach in Division I history to win three hundred games. Still, all the awards in the world could not make up for falling short of the ultimate goal. "Every season, we always felt we'd be competing for a national championship," Juergen Sommer said. "The season was a marathon. It wasn't a sprint. We were preparing for the championship. We learned something from every game and steadily improved. Evansville was such a big rivalry. Losing to them was a hard one to take."

1991: First Big Ten Champs

The 1991 season represented a new beginning for the team. Some outstanding freshmen entered the scene, including Todd Yeagley. Could they provide the offense that IU had been searching for? In 1990 the Hoosiers had managed to score just forty-six goals. They needed a new spark—and they got it, fast. The team's first two games of the season took place on the road. IU opened at Butler, where freshman Blake Rodgers tallied two goals and led the Hoosiers in a 5-0 shutout over the Bulldogs. IU then traveled south to Louisville, posting a 3-0 win. The Hoosiers returned to Bloomington with confidence. They may have had five freshmen in the starting eleven, but they had just

shut out two opponents by a total score of 8-0. Not a bad beginning.

Stanford gave the Hoosiers some trouble in the first match of the adidas-MetLife Classic, and the game ended in a 2-2 draw. Two days later, the Hoosiers faced Penn State. The Nittany Lions put themselves on the board first. With the team down 1-0, a Yeagley took charge. Todd Yeagley stepped up to the challenge, tallying three goals in the match and leading the Hoosiers to a 5-3 win. "I remember my first game ever, going out during the National Anthem, and realizing this has happened," Todd Yeagley said. "I'd always looked out at the team, and now I was part of it. Then I scored three goals against Penn State in the Classic as a freshman. That was a very fond memory." The Big Ten had not acknowledged soccer as a conference sport prior to the '91 season. The game between IU and Penn State was the first-ever conference game.

Determined to build on their 3-0-1 record, the Hoosiers continued to win. They went undefeated in their next ten matches.

Todd Yeagley is leveled by an opponent. During his four years at IU, the Hoosiers dominated competition but never won the national championship. Todd was named Player of the Year in 1994. Photo: Tim Zielenbach, 1992 *Arbutus*.

Goalkeeper Ernie Yarborough hugs Steve Keller after the Hoosiers' 2-1 victory over Penn State in the 1992 Big Ten Championship game. It was IU's second consecutive conference title. Photo Sam Riche, 1993 *Arbutus*.

Then came Wisconsin. Traveling to Madison, the Hoosiers planned on extending their Big Ten unbeaten streak, but the Badgers had other plans. A loose ball collision gave the Badgers a penalty kick, which led to a goal. With a 1-0 lead, Wisconsin fought off the Hoosiers, collecting the victory and ending IU's Big Ten unbeaten streak at sixty-eight games. IU won its next two matches before dropping a 2-1 loss to Yale. With one regular-season match left, IU defeated Harvard 4-0. The Hoosiers then hosted the first Big Ten Tournament. After sitting out the first round, they handed Penn State a 4-2 loss before heading into the final against Wisconsin. Less than a month earlier, the Badgers had upset IU. This time, it would be the Hoosiers' turn. After playing a scoreless first half, IU stepped up to the challenge in the second half. Brandon Ward and Craig Ginsberg scored in a fifteen-minute span, giving IU the 2-0 victory. The Hoosiers had won the inaugural Big Ten Championship.

With a 17-2-2 record, IU headed into the NCAA Tournament as the No. 1 seed. The Hoosiers sat out round one and then faced Wisconsin for the third time that season. The teams went scoreless in regulation, sending the game into overtime. Matt Coyer and Wane Lobring each tallied for IU, giving the Hoosiers a 2-0 victory. IU then welcomed SMU to Armstrong Stadium for a thriller. The teams battled it out for ninety minutes, but no one scored, and this game, too, went into overtime. IU scored twice in the two overtime periods and was sitting pretty with a 2-0 lead. But with just six minutes remaining in the match, SMU tallied two goals, tying the game. Neither team scored in the two fifteen-minute extra periods, sending the game into penalty kicks. After 150 minutes of play, everyone's legs felt like rubber. Luckily, however, IU had some steam left. Mike Clark, Blake Rodgers,

Mike Anhaeuser, and Matt Coyer each netted a PK for IU. Unfortunately, SMU finished all four of their PK attempts as well. Steve Keller came to the line for the Hoosiers. He blasted a shot into the net, giving IU the 3-2 win. The Hoosiers were headed back to the Final Four. In their semifinal match, however, Santa Clara put a damper on the Hoosiers' championship hopes, dominating the game and handing IU a 2-0 loss.

"I joined in 1991 with Todd's class," transfer goalkeeper Andre Luciano said. "I was the old man. I remember Coach asked me if I could help the team win a championship. I said yes. But we lost in the Final Four. As a player you live with that disappointment." The young team ended the season with a 19-3-2 record, seventy goals scored, and hope that the best was yet to come.

1992: Reality Check

With the majority of players returning in 1992, IU looked to come out with a vengeance. But the season started out on a disappointing note. The Hoosiers dropped their first two matches, 1-0 losses to both Duke and UCLA. Worse, they were defeated on their home turf. The loss against Duke snapped IU's thirty-six-game unbeaten streak at Bill Armstrong Stadium, which had dated back to 1989. But that didn't stop the Hoosiers from firing back. IU won its next three matches, destroying Butler, Kentucky, and Akron by scores of 3-0, 6-0, and 1-0. The Hoosiers then ran into a brick wall named St. Louis. The Billikens gave the Hoosiers a taste of their own medicine, shutting them out 2-0.

The Hoosiers won their next three matches, then hit another low point, losing two and tying one. Penn State welcomed IU to Happy Valley and handed the Hoosiers a 3-1 loss, starting IU's streak of bad luck. The Hoosiers then tied Wisconsin-Milwaukee 1-1 and welcomed

Bowling Green to their home turf. In a tight match, Bowling Green pulled off a 2-1 win, breaking a 1-1 tie in the second half. At the end of the Hoosiers' first twelve matches, they had a 6-5-1 record, the worst start in IU history. The squad had hit bottom, and they quickly reenergized, beginning an eleven-game unbeaten streak. They tied Wisconsin 0-0 before slaughtering Northwestern 8-0. IU ended the regular season with two ties, 1-1 vs. San Francisco and 0-0 vs. Florida International.

The Hoosiers were the hosts for the Big Ten Tournament that year. IU defeated Ohio State 1-0 and moved on to face Penn State in the championship match. The Hoosiers handed the Nittany

Lions a 2-1 loss, winning their second consecutive Big Ten Championship.

Taking a 12-5-4 record into NCAA play, IU traveled to the University of Evansville for round-one action. Ninety minutes later, the Hoosiers had easily defeated the Aces, 4-1. "It was a good team, and to play them down there was a very emotionally charged event," Ernie Yarborough said. "I'm starting. It's my first NCAA Tournament game. It was one of those situations where I was ready. We're going to get this done regardless of where we play. We went down and we won. We spanked them. We beat them 4-1."

IU returned home to face Washington in round two. The Hoosiers handed the Huskies a 2-0 loss, courtesy of goals by

Matt Coyer and Brian Maisonneuve, and advanced to the quarterfinals. They next traveled west to face San Diego. It was an even battle for eighty minutes of play. Then San Diego scored twice in the last ten minutes, handing IU a 2-0 loss and putting an end to the Hoosiers' Final Four dreams. "In 1992 things didn't bounce our way," Brian Maisonneuve said. "We still ended up going pretty far. It was a frustrating year. We played good soccer, but the results didn't go our way." IU ended an up-and-down season at 14-6-4. But again, they would be back.

1993: The Wrath of Wisconsin

It was a season in which anything was possible. The Hoosier lineup was full of talent. The players had matured. With two disappointing seasons fresh in mind, it was time to make things happen.

The Hoosiers got the season under way by splitting their first two matches, a 1-0 win over UNLV and a 1-0 loss to Rutgers. The loss would fuel the team as they went on a seventeen-game unbeaten streak, posting eight shutouts. With a 9-1-1 record, IU took to the road for the next four games. The road trip resulted in wins, but they weren't all easy ones.

The Hoosiers kicked off the trip at Bowling Green. They fell behind early in the game, and at the end of the first half, Bowling Green had the advantage 2-1. In the second half, IU came out on fire, tallying four goals on the way to a 5-2 win.

Brian Maisonneuve rests his hands on his knees while Wisconsin celebrates at Armstrong Stadium. Ranked No. 1 for most of 1993, IU fell to the Badgers 1-0 in the third round of NCAA Tournament play. Photo: Robb Hill, 1994 *Arbutus.*

Next up, the Hoosiers ventured to Madison to face conference rival Wisconsin. With the game tied 1-1 and with twelve minutes left in the first half, IU tallied two goals for a 3-1 advantage. In the second half, the Hoosiers increased their lead, adding two more goals and taking the 5-1 victory. They then defeated Northwestern 6-2 and Illinois State 3-1 before returning home to face Ohio State. The Hoosiers sent the Buckeyes back to Columbus with a 7-0 loss. IU then wrapped up the regular season with a trip to Tampa for the South Florida Classic, where the squad collected two more wins. The Hoosiers ended the regular season at 16-1-1.

Returning to Madison for the Big Ten Tournament, IU faced off against Penn State in the semifinals. The Hoosiers had never lost a Big Ten Tourney game, but the Nittany Lions decided that the Indiana streak had gone on long enough, handing IU a 1-0 defeat. Regardless of the conference tournament outcome, the Hoosiers were still at the top of their game with a 16-2-1 record. They entered the NCAA Tournament as the No. 1 seed. The Hoosiers looked flawless in a 6-0 win over Memphis in the second round. They then welcomed Wisconsin to Bloomington for round three. On a day when nothing seemed to go IU's way, the Hoosiers dropped the game 1-0 to the Badgers. Wisconsin had upset their Big Ten rival and the No. 1 seed. "Whenever you don't win the big game, it's disappointing," Mike Clark said. "In 1993 we had the best team in the country. We were looking ahead to playing Virginia and ended up losing to Wisconsin." IU finished the season with a 17-3-1 record, one of the best in team history. Although the season had ended on a sour note, the Hoosiers would be back in 1994, looking to dominate the competition once again.

1994: Number One, without a Doubt

The Hoosiers returned to action in 1994 with high hopes. It would be the last chance for the seniors to win a national championship. IU opened up at home with the adidas-MetLife Classic. The Hoosiers won the first match, shutting out South Carolina 1-0. The next day North Carolina handed the team a 2-1 defeat. That loss turned the Hoosiers into warriors, sending them on a fifteen-game winning streak. A 6-0 victory over Miami of Ohio put them in the right frame of mind. With a 2-1 record, the team exploded offensively, defeating Kentucky 6-1, Akron 10-0, and St. Louis 4-0. After six games, the Hoosiers had a 5-1 record. They had outscored their opponents 28-3 en route to the No. 1 rank in the country.

IU posted a perfect 5-0 record in Big Ten play that year, allowing only Penn State to score—and that was just one goal. The Hoosiers outscored their Big Ten opponents 11-1. They wrapped up the season in Los Angeles at the UCLA Classic, facing Cal State Fullerton in first-day action. The two teams battled to the bitter end. With the game tied at 2-2 at the end of regulation, the Hoosiers headed into their first overtime of 1994. CSF came out on the winning end, tallying a goal in overtime and dealing IU its second loss of the season. Two days later, however, the Hoosiers rebounded with a vengeance when they took on host team UCLA. Todd Yeagley and Brian Maisonneuve each tallied a goal as they led the Hoosiers to a 2-0 victory.

The team took a week off before heading to Columbus, Ohio, for the Big Ten Tournament. Wisconsin gave IU some trouble in semifinal action, but the Hoosiers pulled off a 1-0 victory and moved on to face Penn State in the championship. The Nittany Lions managed to score against IU for the second consecutive time. One goal wasn't enough, however, and the Hoosiers handed Penn State a 3-1 loss. IU became the first Big Ten team to win both the regular-season conference title and the conference championship.

The No. 1 team in the nation headed into NCAA action with a record of 19-2. They had collected fourteen shutouts, destroying everyone in their path. IU received the No. 1 seed and awaited round two. The Hoosiers posted 1-0 victories over Notre Dame and Creighton, then moved on to face Cal State Fullerton. The last time the two teams had met, the Hoosiers had lost. This time, the game was on IU's turf. After a scoreless forty-five minutes, Jeff Bannister tallied early in the second half, giving the Hoosiers a 1-0 lead. Caleb Porter added an insurance goal, and Indiana took the 2-1 win. "The game to make it to the Final Four was such a relief because of the pressure of being ranked No. 1 for the majority of my junior and senior year," Todd Yeagley said. "And winning that game at home against Cal State Fullerton, we knew we were on our way."

IU headed back to Davidson, North Carolina, for the College Cup. First up for the Hoosiers was UCLA. On that day, the team would come together and do exactly what needed to be done. "We beat UCLA in the semifinals 4-1," Brian Maisonneuve said. "We were at the Final Four. Everybody was excited. To play as well as we did was so much fun. That game was a total team effort. It really exemplified what our year was. Everybody did their work to get a good result."

The Hoosiers met Virginia in the NCAA Championship. The Cavaliers came out fast and furious, tallying an early goal. IU spent the remainder of the game trying to close in on the 1-0 score. But Virginia proved to be the only team that would hold IU scoreless in 1994. The loss ended the Hoosiers' season—and a number of careers. "In '94, Coach Yeagley is at the top of his game," Ernie Yarborough said. "Todd is doing great for us. We had great seniors. We were there. It was one of those things. When it didn't happen, it was hollow. Imagine someone dangling in front of you the one thing you've wanted your entire life. And they said, 'You can touch it. You can feel it. You can taste it. You can do whatever you want with it for ninety minutes.' At the end of the ninety minutes they take it away and say you may never get that opportunity again. It's a very hard feeling to explain."

Maisonneuve still looks back on the 1994 season with fond memories. "It was probably the most memorable year of my whole career, from a kid to the World Cup," he said. "It could have been a little better if we had won the whole thing. To lose in the final was really frustrating and upsetting. At least once a week I probably think about that game. You look back on it, and yeah, we don't have a ring, we don't have the title of champions, but what we had that whole year—it was just one of those magical years."

The 1994 season would be the end of an era, as the Hoosiers lost some of the best players the program had ever seen. "We had such a close group of guys," Scott Coufal said. "We all felt it was our path to win a national championship, and it didn't happen. Me being a sophomore, it was difficult because I wanted to win for the juniors and seniors. It was their last chance." But in 1995, they would regroup and come back.

1995: Not Too Bad, but Not Too Good

The Hoosiers had ranked at the top of the polls the two previous seasons. They'd had the best players in the nation. And now they had to start over. It would be a bumpy road, but not an unfamiliar one. The rebuilding years were challenging for Yeagley, but they also had their rewards. "Rebuilding years were some of his most fun years," daughter Yvette said. "He loved the challenge of an unpolished team. He got the most from those. I remember him getting ready for preseason and being more excited in years when it was a rebuilding season. He always said, 'This is going to be a tough year,' but always said it with a smile, as if to say, 'Bring it on.' We always thought 'Yeah, right, you're still going to win.'"

The Hoosiers started out the 1995 season on a mediocre note, tying North Carolina State 1-1. They then beat Boston University 2-0 and Rutgers 1-0 before dropping a game to Kentucky, 2-0. The Hoosiers now had a 2-1-1 record. They had battled three overtimes already in what would become a common occurrence in 1995. IU went on a four-game winning streak before dropping a 2-1 result to conference rival Penn State. The team then won two and lost two before going on a seven-game unbeaten streak, sparked by a 7-0 slaughter of Northwestern. The Hoosiers closed out the regular season at the FIU Southern Bell Classic in Ft. Lauderdale, where they picked up two victories, 2-1 over Charlotte and 1-0 over Florida International.

Next was a trip to East Lansing, Michigan, for the Big Ten Tournament, where the Hoosiers posted a 2-1 victory over Northwestern. On the second day, play was canceled because of bad weather. The league decided that the winners of the semifinal matches would be named co-champions of the tournament. The Hoosiers faced off against Penn State. With the score tied 1-1, two Hoosiers became heroes. Jeff Bannister and J. T. Cerroni each tallied a goal, giving IU the 3-1 win.

The Hoosiers headed home to face Butler in the first round of the NCAA Tournament. IU had slid by the Bulldogs earlier in the season with a 1-0 victory, but this time Butler would be on the winning end. The Hoosiers put on both offensive and defensive pressure. The stellar back line held the Bulldogs to only five shots. One shot proved to be enough, however, and Butler walked away with a 1-0 victory, ending IU's run for the College Cup in round one. "1995 was a rough year," Scott Coufal recalled. "The record was all right, but we lost to Butler in the NCAA Tournament. We were a younger team. We didn't have too many seniors at all. It was a rebuilding year." The Hoosiers ended a mediocre season with a 14-5-2 record. They had scored just thirty-five goals, while allowing thirty.

1996: The Spark Reignites

The Hoosiers needed a spark after the 1995 season. Enter the Ukrainian trio from Rochester. Aleksey Korol, Dema Kovalenko, and Yuri Lavrinenko added to an already solid lineup of talent. IU kicked off its season with the annual adidas-MetLife Classic. The Hoosiers got off on the wrong foot, dropping a 1-0 decision to UCLA. The next day they looked to rebound against Duke, but Mother Nature had other plans. At the half, the teams were tied 0-0 when a severe thunderstorm sent everyone in search of shelter. The game was canceled.

IU next headed to Ft. Wayne for the IPFW–Three Rivers Classic. After a 3-2 win over Marquette and a 1-1 tie with the University of Alabama at Birmingham, the Hoosiers headed home, where they came to life, posting 5-0 and 3-0 wins over

Akron and Notre Dame respectively. "In 1996, when the Ukrainian trio arrived, we felt we were back on track," Gino Di-Guardi said. "We knew in the next year or so we'd be at the level that IU should be at. We opened the floodgates."

The Hoosiers prepared to battle two Big Ten opponents. First up was a match at Michigan State. The Spartans got on the board first, but Kovalenko came through with both the game-tying and game-winning goals, giving IU a 2-1 victory—and Yeagley his 400th career win. IU then battled Penn State to a 0-0 draw, sending the game into overtime. Kovalenko scored for IU in the ninety-seventh minute, but Penn State responded before the end of the overtime period, and the game ended in a 1-1 tie. The Hoosiers returned home to face Miami of Ohio. IU dominated the match, winning 4-0. But the game ended on a sour note when Kovalenko, the team's leading scorer, went down with an ankle injury. The fiery freshman had tallied ten goals in eight games for the Hoosiers, but he would watch the remainder of 1996 from the sidelines.

IU's offense came together in the next game against Butler. The Bulldogs scored in the eighteenth minute, but IU came back strong. Lazo Alavanja, Korol, and Lavrinenko scored before the end of the half, giving the Hoosiers a 3-1 lead. IU held strong in the second half, adding three more goals in an impressive 6-1 win. "I think when Dema was playing, our team's personality was to look for him and he would get the goals we needed," Yeagley said. "When he was no longer there, the personality of the team changed, and the players who'd looked to play to Dema now had to pick up the responsibility themselves. If you could stop Dema, perhaps you could stop a lot of Indiana's attack."

Bowling Green put a stop to IU's offensive streak, handing the Hoosiers a 2-0 loss just three days later. The Hoosiers rebounded immediately, embarking on a ten-game unbeaten streak. IU's conference domination continued, as the team knocked off Wisconsin 1-0 and Northwestern by the embarrassing score of 11-1. The Hoosiers then beat Ohio State 1-0 to win the Big Ten regular-season title. IU wrapped up the season at the Charleston Classic in South Carolina, where the Hoosiers picked up 2-1 and 1-0 victories over Charleston and South Carolina, respectively.

IU then headed into Big Ten Tournament action. The Hoosiers tied Penn State 2-2 but won the penalty kick round, earning a spot in the championship match with Michigan State. IU controlled that final match, shutting out the Spartans 4-0 to take the conference championship.

The Hoosiers took a 13-2-3 record into the NCAA Tournament. In round one, IU defeated Evansville 4-1. Next up, the Hoosiers faced off with Bowling Green. Defender Joey Cavallo and Lavrinenko each tallied for IU, giving the Hoosiers a 2-0 win. The team then traveled to Ft. Lauderdale to face Florida International University. The Hoosiers were fighting the flu as they took the field. They played at a fraction of their ability, falling to FIU 1-0. "1996 was the worst of all four years I played at IU," Dennis Fadeski said. "And we made it to the quarterfinals, where we lost to FIU. Everyone had the flu. Our goalkeeper Scott Coufal saved us in that game." The 1996 season ended with a 15-3-3 record. But the offense had finally ignited, scoring fifty-eight goals. The team would return the majority of its starters in 1997. The possibilities seemed endless.

1997: Breaking Records, Ending in Heartbreak

It had been twenty-five years since Jerry Yeagley and the men's soccer team had gained varsity status. The anniversary season would be one to remember. The Hoosiers were packed with talent. The offense was lethal, the defense solid. Indiana University looked to be the team to beat.

The Hoosiers kicked off the season with a 4-0 domination of Notre Dame in South Bend. A couple of days later, they would have to fight a little harder for a win. The squad traveled back to Bloomington to take on Rutgers in the adidas–Foot Locker Classic. They overcame three one-goal deficits to tie the match at 3-3. Kovalenko scored a goal in the ninety-eighth minute to give IU the 4-3 victory.

That would be the Hoosiers' only close call for a while. They defeated Clemson 3-0 and won their own classic. They then headed out east to the Duke adidas Classic, where they took yet another title, defeating North Carolina State 5-1 and Duke 2-1. "We felt very comfortable," Yuri Lavrinenko said. "The team played well from the start. We had a lot of talent, and we all just clicked."

Next up was the Butler Classic in Indianapolis. The Hoosiers slid by Bowling Green 1-0, then handed Rhode Island a 6-1 win en route to their third straight classic title. IU now had a 7-0 record. After returning home, the Hoosiers faced Kentucky. By the end of their 9-0 domination of the Wildcats, the fans were on their feet. Three days later, IU kicked off the Big Ten season, shutting out Michigan State 3-0. The Hoosiers then welcomed Penn State to their home turf. IU completely shut down Penn State's offense, not allowing the team to take a single shot on the way to a 2-0 Indiana victory. The Hoosiers defeated their other three Big Ten opponents, collecting another clean sheet in conference play. The only Big Ten team to score on IU was Wisconsin, but one goal didn't cause the Hoosiers to flinch, and they collected a 4-1 win.

The Hoosiers closed out the regular season at the California Classic in San Francisco, where they defeated Stanford 2-1 and California 3-1. As the season came to an end, IU was atop the polls and sitting pretty with an 18-0 record. It was the first time a Hoosier team had ended the season with a perfect record.

IU hosted the 1997 Big Ten Tournament. After sitting out round-one action, the Hoosiers faced off against Penn State. This time they doubled their previous score, beating the Nittany Lions 4-0. In the title game against Ohio State, freshman defender Nick Garcia stepped up for IU, tallying the lone goal of the match in the twenty-first minute. On a cold, snowy day in Bloomington, the Hoosiers held off the Buckeyes and held strong, winning their twentieth consecutive game. "1997 was a great team, undefeated throughout the season," Ernie Yarborough said. "Many people argued it was one of the best college teams ever. In '97 you expected somehow, someway we'd win and play in the final."

With a 20-0 record, IU was the undisputed No. 1 seed in the NCAA Tournament. The Hoosiers would enjoy home field advantage until the College Cup. In game one, Indiana faced off against in-state rival Butler. Lazo Alavanja stepped up early for the Hoosiers, sending an early blast into the net for the 1-0 advantage. IU held on to its lead for almost the remainder of the match. With eight minutes left to play, Butler's Craig Donaldson scored, sending the match into overtime. The teams battled through almost three overtime periods before a Hoosier freshman came to the rescue. Matt Fundenberger headed in the winning goal in the 124th minute, giving IU the 2-1 win.

In the next two rounds of NCAA play, IU rolled past Bowling Green 4-0 and then South Florida 6-0. The road had led the Hoosiers directly to the College

Cup in Richmond, Virginia. IU stood tall at 23-0. With two more victories, the Hoosiers would win the NCAA Championship, and Yeagley would end his year at 25-0. Then came UCLA. The Hoosiers and Bruins generally played intense matches, but this one would take that intensity to a new level. It was offense vs. offense and defense vs. defense. Neither team scored in regulation, or in the first overtime, or in the second overtime. The third overtime would send chills down the spines of Hoosier soccer fans everywhere. After 132 minutes of regulation play, UCLA's McKinley Tennyson, an Indianapolis native, netted the only goal of the match, and the Bruins won 1-0. The Hoosiers' luck had run out, and their perfect season came to an end. "1997 was an unbelievable season that ended with a great disappointment," Aleksey Korol said. "It was the best team I've ever played on. We couldn't finish the goals against UCLA. The 1997 team should have won the championship for sure."

Yeagley summed up the season: "It was a special team, it was a special year. They'll go down in the record books, but they'll go down in my book as a very special team and one of the greatest that I've had at IU." That was it—one goal, and IU's flawless season was no more. The Hoosiers had dominated everyone in their path in 1997. They ended with a 23-1 record, posting thirteen shutouts and outscoring their opponents 83-14. "We all sat around and were just dumbfounded," head strength coach Katrin Koch said. "We had such a good hand, and the last card didn't fall for us. The disappointment in their faces . . .

Dema Kovalenko lies on the ground in utter disappointment after the Hoosiers' 1-0 loss to UCLA in the 1997 NCAA semifinals. Photo: Jim Bowling, 1998 *Arbutus*.

I just hugged them. Once you set yourself a goal and you haven't achieved it, there's nothing anybody can say in that moment."

It had been nine years of success, dominance, and pure talent. During that time, IU had some of the most talented teams that college soccer had ever seen. Those teams went 159-30-16 and outscored their opponents 541 goals to 164. Indiana made an appearance in the NCAA Tournament in each of the nine years, including four Final Fours. But those nine years had not brought another national title. Each team had fallen short of its ultimate goal—winning the NCAA Championship. "Some of the best teams we've had didn't win championships," Yeagley recalled. "1979 and 1997—I turn those two numbers around. In 1979 we had eighteen shutouts, more than any team has ever had in NCAA history. In 1997 we had twenty-three wins in a row, more than anybody has ever had in a row. Neither team won the national title. Yet there was no question in my mind or with the top soccer people in the country that we were the best team in the nation. 1984 and 1994 were similar. There were some disappointments. I feel we should have ten titles."

8

The Last Six Years

It had been ten years since the IU soccer program had won a national championship. The Hoosiers' last win, in 1988, had been on their home turf. They'd had plenty of close calls in those years, and the year before they had been only one goal away from the title. The Hoosiers were a team with something to prove.

1998: Putting an End to the Drought

The 1998 season started out on a positive note, as the Hoosiers won their first three matches, including the adidas Classic, and outscored their opponents 9-0. But at the SMU Classic, the host institution gave IU a rude awakening, prevailing 2-1. It was Indiana's first regular-season loss since October 13, 1996. That loss sparked something inside the team, and they steamrollered over their next thirteen opponents. All of their Big Ten opponents fell as the Hoosiers easily won the regular-season conference title.

The No. 1 Hoosiers then faced No. 3 UCLA in the UCLA Soccer Classic. It

Dema Kovalenko jumps on a group of teammates as the Hoosiers celebrate their 1998 NCAA Championship win over Stanford, 3-1. Kovalenko, Aleksey Korol, and Yuri Lavrinenko tallied Indiana's three goals. Photo: Garrett Ewald, 1999 *Arbutus*.

would be a rematch of the 1997 semifinals. As soon as the whistle blew, things started to heat up on the field. UCLA's McKinley Tennyson put the Bruins on the board first. Two minutes later, Dema Kovalenko matched Tennyson's goal. With the score tied 1-1 at intermission, the teams battled even harder in the second half. Just four minutes in, the Bruins scored again. Down by one goal, IU put on the pressure, but failed to finish any attempts. UCLA handed the Hoosiers their second loss of the year. "We were sitting back waiting for things to happen," goalkeeper T. J. Hannig said. "And they didn't. But now we're looking forward to the NCAAs. Hopefully we'll play UCLA again, and then there will be a different result."

IU returned to Bloomington 16-2 and awaited the Big Ten Championships. The Hoosiers sat out round one, but they quickly took control against Wisconsin in round two. The Hoosiers scored four goals in the first half and held on for a 4-0 shutout. They then met Penn State in the finals. The two teams battled for ninety scoreless minutes. Senior Lazo Alavanja scored in the second minute of overtime play, giving IU its seventh Big Ten Championship in eight years. The Hoosiers did not allow their Big Ten opponents to score a single goal in 1998, outscoring them 14-0.

Going into NCAA play, the Hoosiers felt good about their situation. Their record was now 18-2. The team gathered to watch the Big Ten Championship games on television and awaited the NCAA seed announcement. Then Yeagley walked in, turned off the television, and asked for everyone's attention. "Here's the deal— we're a No. 8 seed," he said. Everyone sat in a state of disbelief, humbled by the announcement. "It's disappointing that our strength of schedule index wasn't as

strong this year," Justin Tauber said. "But we're used to tough conditions."

Perhaps the Hoosiers were needing something to light a fire under them. They entered the NCAA Tournament with home field advantage for the first two games. They took both games into overtime, defeating Akron 3-2 and Butler 2-1.

IU then had a challenge to face. The No. 2 Hoosiers would travel east to Clemson, South Carolina, to face the No. 1 ranked Clemson Tigers. This game could end the Hoosiers' run to the Final Four. On a sunny, warm afternoon, the Hoosiers took the field at Clemson. The Clemson fans were out in numbers, ready to cheer their team on to victory. But IU had other plans.

Aleksey Korol shined for the Hoosiers, scoring early. Clemson added a goal before the end of the half. Korol answered that goal just over two minutes into the second half, giving IU a 2-1 lead. The Hoosiers held on for the remainder of the game, finding a way to shut down Clemson's offense. As time ran out, the IU fans rose to their feet and cheered as the Hoosiers advanced to the College Cup. "Clemson was probably the most fun game," Dennis Fadeski said. "It was a good field. Fans were right on top of you. We had six thousand people screaming at us. Aleksey scored both goals. It should have been the national championship game."

IU faced Santa Clara in the semifinal game. The Hoosiers wasted no time in showing the Broncos who was in charge, shutting them out 4-0. Korol scored two goals, and Kovalenko and sophomore defender Nick Garcia each added one.

Two days later, the Hoosiers would play Stanford in their first final since 1994. The team was more fired up then ever. The Ukrainian trio led the offensive burst. Kovalenko scored at the 6:54 mark. Yuri

Lavrinenko tallied a goal just twelve minutes later, giving IU a 2-0 advantage. But in soccer, a 2-0 lead is never safe. Stanford cut the lead to one goal by scoring on a penalty kick. But before the first half came to an end, Korol would step up to the challenge. He sent a blast into the net, giving IU a 3-1 lead. No one scored in the second half, as IU's defense stepped up again and found a way to shut down Stanford's offense.

"In '97 we tasted it," Nick Garcia said. "In '98 we wanted to get back to the final game. We had to go to Clemson, play the No. 1 team, and beat them to advance to the Final Four. After we won, going to the Final Four was icing on the cake."

The Hoosiers had finally proved that they were worthy of the No. 1 ranking, as they won their fourth national championship. A speechless Alavanja celebrated with his teammates on the field. Richmond Stadium, where dreams had been shattered in 1997, was now the stadium where dreams had come true. "It feels splendid," senior midfielder Lazo Alavanja said. "I can't even express it. It's the best feeling ever. Most of us remember how it felt last year. We didn't feel too good, and we didn't want to go through that again."

The 1998 season had been one of true domination. The Hoosiers ended the year with a 23-2 record, having outscored their opponents 63-11, with seventeen shutouts. Statistics spoke volumes about what the Hoosiers had accomplished, but winning that championship mattered most.

1999: Back-to-Back Champions

After winning it all in 1998, the Hoosiers hoped to defend their title in 1999. However, everyone who played them that year had other plans. The Hoosiers expected to do well, but they could not predict how

successful they would be. "1999 was supposed to be a rebuilding year," Lavrinenko said. "We lost a few guys. It was supposed to be a lot tougher. We struggled a little bit the first couple games. And as usual, we turned things around."

That turnaround came quickly. IU started the season with a 1-0 shutout of Maryland, then dropped the next two games, losing to St. Louis and Yale. But in game four of the season, the Hoosiers took on Brown at the Brown/adidas Classic in Providence. IU posted an impressive 5-0 victory over Brown, the start of what would be a thirteen-game winning streak. The Hoosiers defeated every Big Ten opponent in regular-season play on their way to another regular-season conference title.

The Hoosiers sat out round one of the Big Ten Tournament at Michigan State, then faced Northwestern. The game started off slowly, with neither team able to capitalize on opportunities. Lavrinenko finally found a way to get the Hoosiers on the board. He took a freekick after being leveled by a Wildcat, sending it directly into the top right corner of the net. "I looked up and saw a wall of six or seven guys," Lavrinenko said. "I saw the goalie in the center of the net and figured the best place for me to send it was into the far corner. And it worked."

IU held on to the 1-0 lead for the remainder of the half. Matt Fundenberger added a goal in second-half play, giving the Hoosiers a 2-0 advantage. The Wildcats began pressing late in the game, but they failed to get through the Hoosiers' back line. IU won the game and moved on to the championship match with Penn State.

The two teams had battled earlier in the season, and IU had walked away with a 4-2 win. But this time a championship

Pat Noonan and Aleksey
Korol were key players for the
Hoosiers in the 1999 season.
Korol had fifty-seven goals
and thirty-five assists in his
four years at IU; Noonan
tallied forty-eight goals and
thirty-one assists. Photo:
Chris Howell, *The Herald-
Times.*

title was on the line. The conference rivals gave their fans a show. A battle in the midfield failed to allow any goals for the first eighteen minutes of the match, but in the nineteenth minute Penn State took a 1-0 lead. IU answered the goal sixty-one minutes later. Lavrinenko and Fundenberger combined to send the ball to Korol. He headed the ball in, evening the score at one apiece. No one scored in the next ten minutes, and the game went into overtime.

In the second overtime period, Korol prevailed in a one-on-one challenge with the goalkeeper and tallied the second goal of the night, giving the Hoosiers the 2-1 win and an automatic ticket to the NCAA

Tournament. "At the half we told them, 'Right now Penn State deserves to be the champion, but you still have time to change that,'" Yeagley said. "And they did. This was a classic final, with both teams giving it their all and fighting to the end."

It was NCAA Tournament time again. Enjoying home field advantage, the Hoosiers defeated Kentucky in an intense 1-0 overtime win, Washington 2-0, and Penn State 3-0 en route to Charlotte, North Carolina, for the College Cup.

First up for the Hoosiers was long-time rival UCLA. The Bruins had knocked IU out of tourney play in 1997, handing the Hoosiers a 1-0 semifinal loss. Would this game be a repeat? The first half yielded

no goals, but the second half would prove to be a whole different ball game as both teams picked up the pace. IU scored first. At the 54:23 mark, Lavrinenko passed to Ryan Mack. Mack took possession of the ball and moved toward the middle of the field, crossing to Pat Noonan. The ball bounced off of Noonan's chest. He gained control and shot the ball past Bruins keeper Nick Rimando to give IU a 1-0 lead.

Twenty minutes later, the Hoosiers scored again. This time it was Lavrinenko who tallied the goal, giving IU a 2-0 advantage. With less than fifteen minutes on the clock, UCLA put things into overdrive. The Bruins tallied two quick goals, sending the game into overtime. And not just one overtime—the teams battled through almost four extra ses-

sions. At the 141:24 mark, Mack became a Hoosier hero as he sent the ball past a sliding Rimando, giving IU the 3-2 victory. Indiana advanced to the championship game for the second consecutive year. "What a great soccer match," Yeagley said. "I never thought when we had a two-goal lead with fifteen minutes to go that we'd be headed into overtime. But we did. This team has great character, and they find a way to win."

Ryan Mack recalled the UCLA game as his favorite in his IU career. "My most memorable moment was when I scored the game-winning goal vs. UCLA in the semifinals," Mack said. "That's the longest game I've ever played in and the most reward I've ever felt."

In the championship match on Sun-

The Hoosiers celebrate back-to-back NCAA Championships with a 1-0 victory over Santa Clara in the 1999 finals. It was the fifth national title for IU and Coach Yeagley. Photo: IU Athletics.

day, IU faced Santa Clara. The two teams had battled in the semifinals in 1998, with IU walking away with the 4-0 victory. Both teams had gone into quadruple overtime on Friday night and would be playing on less than two days' rest. But if the players were tired, they didn't show it. Santa Clara put on the pressure as soon as the whistle blew. The team registered its first shot just fifty-nine seconds into the match. But IU did not succumb to the pressure. The Hoosiers tallied a goal in the twenty-ninth minute and took a 1-0 lead.

Noonan stole the ball from Santa Clara and sent it upfield to Mack. He forwarded the ball to Lavrinenko, who completed a give-and-go with Korol. Lavrinenko kicked the ball to the left of Santa Clara's goalkeeper, tallying the first goal of the night. The Hoosiers picked up their defense while the Broncos attempted to put on more pressure. Neither team scored in the remainder of the game. A 1-0 lead proved to be enough. The Hoosiers won the game—and the team's fifth national championship. "We both had heavy legs after we both played in four overtimes Friday night," John Swann said. "We got some lucky bounces. They got some lucky bounces. But champions find a way to win."

The Hoosiers ended the decade with a 185-33-14 record, tied with Virginia for the most NCAA Championships, at five. "I can't say that we were the best team in the 1990s," Yeagley said. "But we're the best team in 1999."

2000: Could It Be a Three-Peat?

The 2000 season started on a sour note for the Hoosiers. No one expected the back-to-back NCAA champions to begin the season with two straight losses, but that's exactly what happened. Portland shut them out 3-0, and UCLA then

prevailed 2-1. The next week, IU would finally see the light. The Hoosiers sneaked past Maryland 2-1 in overtime, earning their first victory of the season. They went on to win thirteen of their next fourteen matches, losing only to Creighton, 4-1.

The Hoosiers ended the regular season the way they had started it, losing two straight games. However, they again won the Big Ten regular-season title, having defeated all their conference opponents. In round one of the Big Ten Tournament, IU faced Ohio State on the Buckeyes' home turf. The Buckeyes surprised IU, winning 1-0. The Hoosiers were knocked out of the tournament for the first time since 1993. Their Big Ten winning streak came to an end at thirty-eight games.

IU's record now stood at 13-6, barely above the .500 mark. Nevertheless, the Hoosiers slid into the tournament, where they became road warriors. "We almost expected to go back to the Final Four," Tyler Hawley said. "After we lost to OSU in the Big Ten Championships in 2000, everyone had their heads down. Yeagley said, 'We're not going to make it.' He knew we were going to get into the tournament, but that just pushed us harder once we made it in."

The Hoosiers went on the road, traveling across the country en route to another Final Four. The 2000 season was the first time since 1992 that IU had not kicked off the NCAAs at home. Nevertheless, the Hoosiers took charge. "We had a lot of challenges in 2000," Assistant Coach Mike Freitag said. "We didn't take care of business in the regular season like we should have. We had to take the hard road. In this program, sometimes when the hill is a little higher, we take bigger steps to get there."

IU steamrollered over the eighth seed, San Jose State, 4-0. The Hoosiers had scored only one goal in their prior three

games, but that scoring drought was now at an end. Pat Noonan, Matt Fundenberger, John Swann, and Ryan Mack each tallied a goal in the Hoosiers' impressive win. "I'm very pleased with our play today," Yeagley said. "Recently we haven't been able to finish on our scoring opportunities, but it seemed as if we cleaned that up quite well today. Our confidence and veteran experience are also important when reaching tournament play."

The Hoosiers then traveled back out west to play Washington, handing the Huskies a 2-1 loss. The following week, IU headed east to face the No. 1 seed in the nation, North Carolina. The odds were against them, but the Hoosiers came out fighting. Both teams battled for control of the match, but no one could score

in the first half. When the teams took the field after intermission, they increased their intensity. North Carolina took fourteen shots in the half, while the Hoosiers took just six. When Ryan Mack tallied a goal at the 58:52 mark, the Hoosiers took a 1-0 lead and never looked back. The Tar Heels failed to capitalize, and IU was headed to its fourteenth College Cup. "In 2000, we almost traveled across the world," Noonan said. "We played at San Jose, Washington, and North Carolina and won all those games. It was a pretty long postseason."

In the semifinals of the College Cup, IU would face Creighton. Earlier in the season, the Bluejays had beaten IU 4-1. But on this evening in Charlotte, North Carolina, it would be a fight to the finish.

Armstrong Stadium was given a facelift in 2000. The grandstand and the press box facilities on the north side were torn down. The hill on the south side became home to a new 5,000-seat concrete grandstand and new press box facilities. The stadium also received improved lighting and a new grass playing field. Photo: Paul Riley, IU Athletics.

Both teams had something to gain. If the Hoosiers won, they would play in their third consecutive championship game. If Creighton won, the Bluejays would make their first trip to the championship game.

Pat Noonan put the Hoosiers on the board in the thirtieth minute. Creighton's Brian Mullan scored early in the second half, evening the score at 1-1. Neither team capitalized on chances for the remainder of regulation. In overtime, the Bluejays stepped up their offensive pressure. For a while, the Hoosiers had luck on their side. Two attempts bounced off the post in the first overtime period. The third attempt, however, would be a different story. In the 125th minute of play, another ball bounced off the post. Creighton's Mike Tranchilla fought for the rebound. He sent it into the net, ending the game with a 2-1 win.

"In 2000 we played the regular-season No. 1, the Pac-10 Champion, and the No. 1 seed in the tournament," head strength coach Katrin Koch said. "And how much fun was that! Losing to Creighton wasn't good. But making it there was a huge achievement."

2001: Falling Two Goals Short

After their disappointing finish in 2000, the Hoosiers came out ready for action in 2001. But they would do it without two key players. Both Ryan Mack and freshman Ned Grabavoy had suffered injuries that kept them on the sidelines. Indiana dropped the first game of the season 2-1 to St. John's. But the Hoosiers rebounded the next night with a 1-0 double-overtime win against Kentucky.

The Hoosiers then headed out west to the Portland Classic. They split the trip, with a 1-0 win over Washington and a 1-0 loss to Portland. IU returned to Bloomington with a record of 2-2. "We didn't look like a championship group in the early weeks of the season," Yeagley said.

"We were working on putting the pieces in the different places they needed to go. Different people stepped into new roles and filled the gaps we needed to fill."

And then the Hoosiers returned to the Midwest and traveled to Louisville. IU handed the Redbirds an impressive 4-0 loss and began a seven-game winning streak. In the middle of that streak, IU welcomed in-state rival Butler. The Hoosiers easily took care of the Bulldogs, handing them a 3-0 loss. The victory also marked a milestone for Yeagley, as he won his 500th game. "The honor goes to everyone who has ever worn a uniform, any coach, any support staff, and everyone who has supported Indiana soccer," Yeagley said. "Five hundred games do not seem that long ago. I can still remember the first one."

Notre Dame put an end to IU's unbeaten streak, defeating the Hoosiers 1-0 on their home field. IU bounced right back, going on an unbeaten streak for the remaining four games of the regular season. In the final game of the season, the Hoosiers handed IUPUI a 6-0 loss. It was not a bad ending after such a rocky beginning.

Going into Big Ten play, IU had a record of 12-3-1. The Hoosiers again won the regular-season conference title, before heading to Wisconsin for the Big Ten Tournament. They were looking to avenge their early exit in 2000. IU and Michigan battled in the semifinals of the tournament. After triple overtime, Indiana came away with a 1-0 win, courtesy of a Pat Noonan goal. In the championship match, the Hoosiers faced Michigan State. The two teams battled the brisk Wisconsin weather, with IU taking the 2-0 victory.

When the NCAA brackets were announced, the Hoosiers received a No. 4 seed, and again they would host tournament action. First up was conference rival Michigan State. It was the third meeting of the season for the two teams, and it proved to be their most intense battle. At the end of a full ninety minutes, the Hoosiers had prevailed 1-0, thanks to a penalty kick by Tyler Hawley in the twelfth minute. The Hoosiers advanced to the next round.

Rutgers traveled to Bloomington for the next tournament game. It was the teams' second meeting in 2001. The Hoosiers walked away with an easy 3-0 win. "When we played at Rutgers, they were really pumped up," Hawley said. "They thought they had our number. We just came in, and like clockwork, we just killed them. They came to our field for the tournament three weeks later, and we beat them 3-0."

Last but not least, IU welcomed Clemson to Armstrong Stadium. The Hoosiers handed the Tigers a 2-0 loss en route to their fifteenth College Cup. In semifinal action, the Hoosiers would again face a team for the second time in the season. IU had played St. John's in the season opener, which the Red Storm had won 2-1. This time, IU planned to come away with the victory.

No one scored in the first half, but the second half was a different story. The Red Storm quickly got on the board, scoring at the 49:03 mark. Less than twenty minutes later, Mike Ambersley evened the game at 1-1. Neither team scored in the remaining minutes, and the game moved into overtime—and not just one overtime; it was the second extra period when Vijay Dias sent a shot over St. John's keeper for the 2-1 win.

For the third time in four years, the Hoosiers were in the championship game and facing North Carolina. The year before, IU had knocked the Tar Heels out of the tournament, but this time the Tar Heels set the tone of the match early, scoring on just their second shot of the match, taking a 1-0 lead. "We played well

early on," Freitag said. "We had the better of it. Their first goal was the one that hurt us. After that, the momentum swung in their direction."

IU failed to answer the goal, and with just fifteen minutes remaining in the game, North Carolina sent a penalty kick into the net, for a 2-0 advantage. Again the Hoosiers could not capitalize on their chances, and the Tar Heels won the championship, 2-0. "When we lost to North Carolina, on that day North Carolina was the better team," John Swann said. "We were supposed to win that game. We were the better team. But at the end of the day, the scoreboard didn't show it."

Pat Noonan talked about his disappointment. "It was always tough, but they were great runs," Noonan said. "In 2001, we played with a talented team, but a weaker IU team, and we made it to the Final Four. Coming in second is never easy."

2002: Exiting Early

The 2002 season started out on a mediocre note as the Hoosiers tied their first two matches in the annual adidas Classic, 0-0 with Rutgers and 1-1 with Clemson. "We played well defensively and really answered some questions," Yeagley said after the Clemson game. "We expected our offense to be strong, but it kind of sputtered, and that will happen. Again, I was pleased with our performance, but we can't be satisfied with not winning."

The Hoosiers struggled to score in those two games. That came as a surprise to many, since IU had one of the top offenses in the country, with Pat Noonan, Ryan Mack, and Ned Grabavoy. Noonan and Mack were both preseason All-Americans and Hermann Trophy candidates. Perhaps it would take a few games for things to gel.

The Hoosiers traveled out east for the St. John's Classic, hoping that maybe their

luck would change. And for one game, it did. IU handed William & Mary a 2-1 loss on day one of the Classic. But in the final game, St. John's shut out IU 3-0. The loss was what the Hoosiers needed to kick their game into high gear. They went on an eleven-game winning streak. They won big against two conference opponents, 6-1 over Michigan State and 5-1 over Wisconsin. They also managed to go undefeated in Big Ten play, earning their seventh consecutive regular-season conference title. Out of the thirty-nine goals that IU scored in 2002, twenty were scored against Big Ten opponents.

IU received a No. 1 ranking, just in time for a trip out to Cal State Fullerton. Unfortunately, that's where the winning streak came to an end. The Titans handed IU a 2-1 loss. Two days later, the Hoosiers faced UC Santa Barbara. Led by Pat Noonan's two goals, they picked up the pace. Michael Bock added a third goal for IU as the team defeated UCSB 3-1. The Hoosiers returned home and slid past IUPUI in double overtime with a 2-1 win.

The Hoosiers then packed their bags and headed to State College, Pennsylvania, for the Big Ten Tournament. After sitting out round one, they would face the host institution, Penn State. Earlier in the season it had taken two overtimes for IU to defeat the Nittany Lions. History came close to repeating itself.

Indiana's Mike Ambersley scored in the sixteenth minute, giving the Hoosiers a 1-0 advantage. IU sat on that lead for most of the match. With forty-eight seconds showing on the clock, Penn State tied it up, sending the game into overtime. Neither team scored in overtime, and the game went into penalty kicks.

The Hoosiers missed their first two attempts, while Penn State made theirs. With IU down 2-0, Vijay Dias stepped

up to the line. He shot—and scored. Penn State tallied. IU's Brian Plotkin countered. The score was now 3-2. If the Nittany Lions made the next shot, they would win the match. Penn State proved lethal, eliminating IU from the Big Ten Championships. "I am proud of our team," Yeagley said. "We should hold our heads up high. It's better for us to lose one now than in the NCAA Tournament."

IU took a 14-3-2 record into NCAA Tourney play. The Hoosiers received a bye in the first round and would host Notre Dame at home. The two Indiana teams battled for the first forty-five minutes, with no one able to score. In the second half, IU took charge. At the 51:03 mark, Big Ten Freshman of the Year Brian Plotkin sent a blast into the back of the net, giving IU the 1-0 advantage. It proved to be enough, as IU took the victory. "The goal helped us break the game open," Plotkin said. "Throughout the season I have been struggling with my shot. It was only a matter of time, though. Tonight it felt good to help out the team."

The Hoosiers then headed east to play the seventh-seeded University of Connecticut. The Huskies found a way to take control of the game. At the 16:35 mark, UConn's Cesar Cuellar found the back of the net, giving his squad a 1-0 advantage. The Hoosiers struggled to get back in the game, but failed on every attempt. "We had all the talent to win every game, but didn't have the right mind frame," Danny O'Rourke said. "It felt like we always thought we were the best, but didn't show it. And that showed in the final game against Connecticut. We had a lot of talent, and it was a fun year. It was a great year, but we came up short."

The Hoosiers fell short of expectations in 2002, exiting the NCAAs in the third round. For the first time in five years, IU would not make a College Cup ap-

Coach Yeagley and Assistant Coach Mike Freitag watch another successful Hoosier match. After Yeagley retired, Freitag became only the second head coach in the history of IU men's varsity soccer. Photo: IU Athletics.

The Hoosiers celebrate after defeating Penn State in penalty kicks to win their tenth Big Ten Championship in 2003. They went on to win their sixth NCAA Championship. Photo: Paul Riley, IU Athletics.

pearance. Assistant Coach Mike Freitag summed up the season with a simple statement. "We underachieved," he said.

2003: Six-Time Champions

The Hoosiers started off the 2003 season with their worst record ever, 2-3-4. They then began a seventeen-game unbeaten streak en route to their sixteenth College Cup appearance. "I think that we believed in ourselves from the start, even though we had the worst start in IU history," Jordan Chirico said. "We just took it one game at a time. We had a young team, and it took some time to gel. And when it

happened, it was amazing. In the beginning of the season, the bounces weren't going our way. We couldn't get that goal in the last five minutes. At the end of the season, everything fell into place."

On the way to the College Cup, the Hoosiers won their tenth Big Ten Championship with a penalty-kick victory over Penn State. They then defeated Kentucky and Virginia Commonwealth before taking to the road for the quarterfinals of the tournament. In Los Angeles the Hoosiers faced off against the No. 1 team in the nation, UCLA. The Hoosiers handed the Bruins a 2-1 loss, then headed to Columbus, Ohio, for the Final Four. At the College Cup, IU defeated Santa Clara 1-0 in the semifinals and St. John's 2-1 in the finals. When the last whistle blew, the Hoosiers celebrated as snow fell on the field. They had won their sixth national championship.

Jerry Yeagley became the first coach in Division I history to win six titles at the same institution. "It was definitely a storybook ending," Danny O'Rourke said. "We started off so poorly. I remember thinking to myself, this has never happened. We're always good at the beginning of the season. It was just frustrating because it's not like we were playing bad. We were playing some good soccer. We just couldn't put the pieces together. We couldn't finish our chances. And we just got unlucky."

Freshman defensive standout Julian Dieterle agreed: "I don't think we could have scripted a better season. After the St. John's game, Coach Yeagley gave us a speech, telling us why our championship was special. That was the icing on the cake. I can't wait to get back out there."

With the final whistle, Jerry Yeagley ended his coaching career. The team had won its tenth Big Ten and sixth NCAA Championship. And the 2003 adidas/ National Soccer Coaches Association of America (NSCAA) Coach of the Year ended his career as the winningest coach ever in Division I history, with a 544-101-45 (.821) record in his thirty-one years at IU. He truly went out on top. It was a storybook ending for a legendary coach. Yeagley's legacy will not be forgotten.

Key Players

Every Hoosier soccer player over the years has contributed to the success of IU's program, but the team has produced a number of key players whose names are well known and respected throughout the soccer world. Some went on to play professional soccer, while others chose professions of another kind, but each left his mark during his time at IU. From Umit Kesim, the first club All-American under Yeagley, to 2003's Ned Grabavoy, the key players for IU reflect the very best that Hoosier soccer has to offer.

When asked who his favorites were, Yeagley would never say. "Each championship is special in its own way," he said. "Each team has its own personality. And the pride that the alums have, I'd be shot if I ever chose one team or one player. So many of them were good. And each one is special in its own way."

The key players stood out. The forwards could dribble around the toughest defenders and score seemingly impossible goals. The midfielders could send a rocket from forty yards out directly into the net. The defenders could shut down all comers, including the nation's top scorers. The goalkeepers could make spectacular diving saves and stop penalty kicks. With their legendary skills, these athletes could have played in any decade. There is room for all of them in the hearts of IU soccer fans.

Fifty-one Hoosiers were named All-Americans in Yeagley's forty-one years at IU. The All-Americans span three decades and represent every position on the field, from forward to goalkeeper. The Hoosiers had three All-Americans before soccer was even a varsity sport at IU: Umit Kesim (1966), Karl Schmidt (1967), and Bob Nelson (1972). Tom Redmond was the first varsity All-American, in 1974. With the exception of the 1975, 1986, and 1995 seasons, IU had at least one player named to an All-American team every year thereafter. Ned Grabavoy would be Yeagley's final All-American, in 2003.

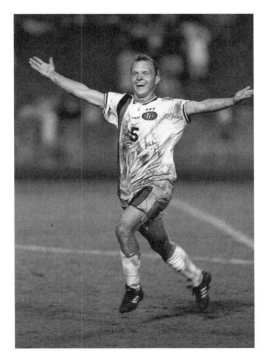

Facing page: Paul DiBernardo had a successful four-year campaign in Bloomington from 1981 to 1984. He ended his career with forty goals and thirty-six assists for 116 career points. Photo: IU Athletics.

Yuri Lavrinenko celebrates after scoring a goal. Lavrinenko led the Hoosiers to back-to-back championships in 1998 and 1999. He ended his four-year career with twenty-five goals and forty-one assists. Photo: IU Athletics.

Angelo DiBernardo was the first Hoosier
to win a Hermann Trophy, which he was
awarded for his performance in 1978.
Photo: IU Athletics.

INDIANA ALL-AMERICANS

First team unless designated

1966	Umit Kesim
1967	Karl Schmidt
1972	Bob Nelson
1974	Tom Redmond (2nd team)
1976	Steve Burks
1977	Angelo DiBernardo George Perry (Honorable Mention) David Shelton
1978	Angelo DiBernardo Charlie Fajkus
1979	Armando Betancourt Mike Freitag
1980	Robert Meschbach Armando Betancourt (2nd team)
1981	Armando Betancourt
1982	John Stollmeyer (2nd team)
1983	Joe Schmid (2nd team)
1984	Paul DiBernardo (3rd team) John Stollmeyer (3rd team)
1985	John Stollmeyer (3rd team)
1987	Ken Snow
1988	Ken Snow
1989	Ken Snow Chad Deering (3rd team)
1990	Ken Snow Chad Deering
1991	Todd Yeagley (2nd team)
1992	Todd Yeagley (2nd team)
1993	Brian Maisonneuve (2nd team) Todd Yeagley (2nd team)
1994	Brian Maisonneuve Todd Yeagley Mike Clark (3rd team)
1996	Lazo Alavanja (2nd team) Scott Coufal (3rd team)
1997	Dema Kovalenko Lazo Alavanja (2nd team) Nick Garcia (3rd team)
1998	Dema Kovalenko Lazo Alavanja Nick Garcia (2nd team)
1999	Aleksey Korol Nick Garcia Yuri Lavrinenko
2000	Pat Noonan (2nd team) Ryan Mack (3rd team)
2001	Pat Noonan
2002	Pat Noonan John Swann Ned Grabavoy (2nd team)
2003	Ned Grabavoy

The Hoosiers earned other awards as well. Five were named National Player of the Year: Angelo DiBernardo, Armando Betancourt, Ken Snow, Brian Maisonneuve, and Todd Yeagley. DiBernardo capped off a successful career at IU in 1978 by winning the Hermann Trophy. In his three years as a Hoosier, he tallied fifty-four goals and seventeen assists for 125 points. But according to DiBernardo, he was just lucky. "As Coach has always said, 'Angelo, you were in the right place at the right time.' That was my job," DiBernardo said. "Your college years are your best years. Soccer made it that much better. Coach Yeagley made it that much better for all of us."

Three years later, Armando Betancourt

Ken Snow is the Hoosiers' all-time leading scorer. He won four National Player of the Year awards and was the team's first four-time All-American. His twenty-eight goals in 1987 still mark an all-time high for IU players. Photo: IU Athletics.

The Hoosiers' all-time leading scorer, Ken Snow, captured four awards in his four years at IU. In both 1988 and 1990, he won the Hermann Trophy and was named Missouri Athletic Club Player of the Year. Snow leads the IU record books in a number of categories. He registered eighty-four goals and twenty-four assists for 196 points. He was the first Hoosier to be named All-American for four consecutive seasons. "I learned soccer watching IU play," *Herald-Times* reporter Andy Graham said. "I think they taught me well. The skill level was very high, and they attempted to play beautiful soccer."

In 1994, the Hoosiers dominated competition. They fell just short of winning it all, but two players stood out and received national recognition that year. Brian Maisonneuve earned the Hermann Trophy after an impressive campaign. In his four years at IU, he collected forty-four goals and twenty-two assists for 110 points. Maisonneuve recalls his teammates with great fondness. "The guys that Coach Yeagley had on his team the four years I was there were class guys," Maisonneuve said. "They were so much fun to hang out with no matter what we did. Even if it was study hall, we had fun."

Sharing the spotlight in 1994 was Todd Yeagley, who was named Missouri Athletic Club Player of the Year. In his four-year stint as a Hoosier he tallied twenty-nine goals and forty assists for ninety-eight points. Yeagley became the second four-year All-American in varsity history. As the coach's son, he believes that his future was almost mapped out for him. "I guess you could say my heroes growing up were the IU players," Todd Yeagley said. "They are who I saw on a regular basis. Those were the people I wanted to be like. It made me want to play soccer. I was always in a unique environment, and soccer was always a part of it."

DiBernardo and Betancourt are also in

became the second Hoosier to win the Hermann Trophy. In his three years at IU, he collected sixty-four goals and thirty-seven assists for 165 career points. Betancourt said he wouldn't have been nearly as successful if it weren't for the soccer environment. "The people who have been around here are real competitors," he said. "They're winners. Sometimes you find people who want to play. But players here are competitors, gladiators in spirit. They're out there to win. They do their best. That's what it takes to have a good program."

the IU Athletic Hall of Fame, along with John Stollmeyer, who attended IU from 1982 to 1985. Stollmeyer was a three-time All-American who helped his team win back-to-back championships in 1982 and 1983. In his four years at Indiana, he netted twenty-seven goals and tallied thirty-nine assists for ninety-three career points. "We set the new standard," Stollmeyer said. "The club guys started it all. There were some great teams that should have won. After we won, we said, 'We are the team you talk about.' Then we won again and went unbeaten. We were the team that made the dynasty. I never said a team was better than mine until I watched the 1997 team. They were fun to watch. In the end there are a lot of players that started this thing. We kept the standard rising."

Stollmeyer is unique in being the only defender among the Hoosier Hall of Famers. "You go back to Bob Jones and then come to Robert Meschbach, Angelo and Paul DiBernardo, Armando Betancourt —any number of them were always so great to watch," Chuck Crabb said. "But there was always the great defense that was played by Indiana soccer. When you think of the number of shutouts, the performances. John Stollmeyer could take over a game and rule the back line."

The players enjoy the respect of the fans, the coaching staff, and, most important, their fellow players. "I was fortunate to be on the team that made the first final in 1976," George Perry said. "Playing with guys like Angelo DiBernardo, Charlie Fajkus, Dave Shelton, Steve Burks—all these guys were just phenomenal. I know that a number of those guys, if you roll forward about twenty to twenty-five years, could still be playing. I was fortunate to be around guys like that."

IU raked in the conference awards as well. Despite being one of eleven Big Ten teams, the Hoosiers dominated conference competition throughout Yeagley's

tenure. Brian Maisonneuve, Lazo Alavanja, Aleksey Korol, Ryan Mack, and Pat Noonan earned Big Ten Player of the Year awards. Todd Yeagley, Lazo Alavanja, Dema Kovalenko, Nick Garcia, Mike Ambersley, Brian Plotkin, and Jed Zayner earned Big Ten Freshman of the Year honors. Yeagley was named Coach of the Year eight times.

John Stollmeyer was known for his ability to shut down an opposing team's offense. He was strong offensively, too, tallying twenty-seven goals and twenty-nine assists in his four years at Indiana. He was elected to the IU Athletics Hall of Fame in 1999. Photo: IU Athletics.

Todd Yeagley was IU's second four-time All-American. He had a stellar freshman season in 1991, with twelve goals and eleven assists. As a senior, he was named the Missouri Athletic Club's Player of the Year. Photo: IU Athletics.

was a strange season in 1984 because the pro league folded in the middle of the year, and those guys kind of felt a big letdown," John Trask said. "Having said that, we continued the winning streak that was part of the forty-six-game unbeaten streak that's still intact."

When the World Cup came to the United States in 1994, another men's professional league was in the works. In 1996, Major League Soccer became a reality. Four Hoosiers—Mike Clark, Brian Maisonneuve, Brandon Ward, and Todd Yeagley—were selected in the original MLS draft, and they all made the cut. All four played for the Columbus Crew. "With the World Cup coming in 1994, we knew there would be a pro league coming because that was part of the agreement to get the World Cup," Todd said. "That was when the silver lining was starting to form again, and I could see the pot of gold at the end of the rainbow. I realized there was a new life for me. I always say how lucky my generation was. There were so many players in the mid-'80s that missed that window between NASL and MLS that were extremely talented, very good players who didn't have a place to play. We were lucky."

Since 1996, a number of former IU players have played at least briefly for MLS. Pat Noonan joined the New England Revolution in 2003 and was a finalist for MLS Rookie of the Year. Also in 2003, Dema Kovalenko made a switch from the Chicago Fire to D.C. United. He was voted D.C.'s Honda MVP for his 2003 performance. Others who saw MLS action include Lazo Alavanja, Scott Coufal, Chad Deering, Nick Garcia, Chris Klein, Aleksey Korol, Yuri Lavrinenko, Caleb Porter, and Juergen Sommer. Former Hoosiers have also played in the A-League (minor league) and the MISL (Major Indoor Soccer League).

Continuing Success

Yeagley's players pursued many careers after their playing days at Indiana were over. Some became doctors, lawyers, and successful businessmen. Others became coaches. But a select group of Hoosiers went on to play professional soccer, both in Europe and in the United States. IU soccer has actually outlived some U.S. professional leagues. The North American Soccer League was disbanded in 1984. "It

A select group of Hoosiers have repre-

Armando Betancourt tallied more than fifty points in each of his three seasons at IU. He was a three-year All-American. He was awarded the Hermann Trophy for his outstanding performance in 1981. Photo: IU Athletics.

sented their alma mater while playing for the United States or for their home country's national team. Angelo DiBernardo and Armando Betancourt became the first two Hoosier Olympians in 1980. DiBernardo represented the United States in Moscow, while Betancourt represented his home country, Honduras. Each year from 1980 to 1996, an Indiana alum made the Olympic roster. Among them were Gregg Thompson, John Stollmeyer, Steve Snow, and Brian Maisonneuve. In 1996, Maisonneuve led the U.S. team in scoring.

Betancourt was the first Hoosier to

Brian Maisonneuve had a slow start to his Hoosier career, tallying just five goals and two assists as a freshman. But by his senior year in 1994, he was among the best in the nation. He earned the Hermann Trophy that year after registering fourteen goals and eight assists in his senior season.
Photo: IU Athletics.

appear in a World Cup, in 1982, playing for Honduras. He was followed by Stollmeyer in 1990, and then Juergen Sommer in 1994. Chad Deering and Brian Maisonneuve joined Sommer in 1998, so that year there were three former Hoosiers representing the United States on the world stage. "It was a symbol to Coach Yeagley in the '98 World Cup when Brian Maisonneuve and I started in the center midfield," Chad Deering said. "It symbolized what IU soccer could produce. It was a shame that Juergen didn't get a chance to get in. But three players out of twenty-three on the national team were out of Indiana. That says something. You look at all the players who are now represent-

ing Indiana on the national team. It's a tribute to him as far as developing as players, but also as people."

The success the players had at IU has carried over into the rest of their lives. As members of the team, they learned to strive to take things to the next level. In addition to the knowledge they gained about soccer and success, they may have learned even more about life. Many of them say they owe a lot to their mentor. "You can't say enough about Coach Yeagley," Kovalenko said. "He's a great person, a great coach, a great motivator, just a good person to be around. He has a great family. Everything he has, he deserves."

10

Defense Wins Championships

en Big Ten Championships. Six NCAA Championships. These two feats were accomplished by a team from the cornfields of Indiana, led by a coach named Jerry Yeagley. The coach, his assistant coaches, and the players were guided by a simple philosophy—defense wins championships. Not until the players had the defense down pat would they focus on scoring. That philosophy proved as successful as the defense itself, as IU dominated Big Ten opponents, becoming the only team to win ten conference titles, and Yeagley became the first coach to win six NCAA Championships at one school.

"Individually and collectively, we've been solid defensively," Assistant Coach Mike Freitag said. "It's the common thread that's been there for thirty-one years of varsity status. People sometimes think if you talk about defending, it's negative. It's not negative. It's half of the game or more. In the same breath, if you can get your team to defend well in practice, you're going to get a better offense."

The foundation for Yeagley's emphasis on defense was laid in the club days. Back then the Hoosiers were trying to compete with the best teams in the country, and they were doing it with not a lot of talent. They had to make up for their shortcomings by concentrating on the basics of the game, primarily transition and defense. "I've always felt very strongly

that to be an effective team, we had to be as good or better defensively than our opponents," Yeagley said. "We worked extremely hard on the transition part of the game and on individual team defending. We take pride, and always have, in our individual and team defending. We've established a lot of records along those lines. We worked very hard on it in practice. Whereas other teams might spend a lot more time on the offense and hope the defense works."

In the Hoosiers' six NCAA Championship seasons, they dominated their opponents statistically. IU posted a 122-15-13 record in those six seasons, recording eighty-five shutouts. Offensively, IU also dominated during those years, outscoring opponents 371-85. The defense held strong, and the offense worked hard to make things happen.

"Something I've always believed is if you don't get scored on, you can't lose," Danny O'Rourke said. "We stress that, whether it's individual defending to not get beaten or good team defending. We work so hard at practicing to become a unit back there. With Coach Yeagley stressing the pressure and the pride of being IU, all that mixed together with the talent we have on this team makes our defense probably the best annually."

IU has dominated the Big Ten Championships since the conference tourna-

ment started in 1991. The Hoosiers have an 18-2-3 record against opponents in conference championship play, and they have won ten of the thirteen championships to date. IU is definitely the driving force in the Big Ten.

Other teams know that when they play IU, they will have to push their offense extra-hard. The Hoosier back line seemed impenetrable during the Yeagley years. Not too many opponents got through that line, and when they did, the goalkeeper was waiting to make the save. "When we play against teams that don't defend as well, it's easier," Freitag said. "It goes hand in hand. We want to play attractive attacking soccer. I think some coaches think you have to do one or the other. We want to be able to do both. That's the ultimate, to defend and also attack. In recent years we've done that really well."

Everyone on the team was drilled in the defensive principles, including the forwards and midfielders. "They teach us to play team defense, which means our pressure and our defense starts with our forwards," O'Rourke said. "It's a whole team effort. I think our team defense was the best in the country." Some players had never played defense until they stepped foot in Bloomington, and many of them were intimidated at first. Defense was emphasized strongly in their daily practices. "Going to IU was the best thing that could have happened to me," Dema Kovalenko said. "I was not ready for the level I'm playing at now. They got me ready. I didn't like to play defense. I was always scared."

Defending is often a foreign concept for forwards. They are the protected players, the speedy players who get the job done. They slip in behind defenders and tally a goal or two. But at IU, they learned that defense could make them stronger players. "When I trained overseas, they

Facing page: Nick Garcia heads the ball out of danger in the 1997 semifinal vs. UCLA. Despite an impressive defense, IU fell to the Bruins 1-0. Photo: Garrett Ewald, 1998 *Arbutus.*

Scott Coufal stops an opponent's attempt to score a goal. Coufal was the only Hoosier goalkeeper to be named an All-American. His sixty-six wins rank first on the Hoosiers' all-time list. Photo: IU Athletics.

couldn't believe that a forward would actually play defense," Tyler Hawley said. "All the other guys were standing around, and I was in my stance ready to defend. The other forwards looked at me like 'What are you doing?'"

As the players' defensive skills got

Defensive back Mike Clark secured the Hoosiers' back line from 1991 to 1994. He was part of a stellar defense that allowed just thirteen goals in both 1993 and 1994. Photo: IU Athletics.

enced only one losing season in his ten club years. The Hoosiers raked in the awards as teams and individually. And at the end of the day, no one could deny that IU was one of the best teams in the nation.

"I'm most proud of the fact that we have had a consistent standard and level over the forty-one years, including the club years," Yeagley said. "The thing I'm most proud of is that we've never dropped our standard. We've somehow been able to maintain a standard of excellence. And that shows in our winning percentage. That's what I'm most proud of. If you coach long enough, you can get any number of wins. Over the years that we've been varsity, we've by far had the best winning percentage. We've played year in and year out as tough a schedule as anyone. We haven't won easy. We schedule tough. I take great pride for all the players who have done that over the thirty-one years. That to me is much more important than any number of wins."

Indiana made it into the NCAA Tournament twenty-eight times under Yeagley, posting a 68-22 record in those games. The Hoosiers reached sixteen Final Fours, and won six national championships.

In conference competition, IU's opponents didn't even have a chance. In the thirteen seasons after the Big Ten recognized men's soccer as a sport and began keeping records, IU dominated. In sixty-nine games, the Hoosiers compiled a 62-4-3 record, outscoring their opponents 204 to 38. "IU always plays hard, and opponents have to play equally as hard," referee Steve Siomos said. "If you beat IU, you know you're a good team. They are hard games to officiate because they are challenging. I always remind referees they'd better be ready for a challenge, especially in Big Ten games."

Some seasons it took a while for IU's defense to come together. The team of-

stronger, the offense would always show up. "In preseason we start on one-on-one defending," Dennis Fadeski said. "We spend a whole week focusing on defense. With the players they bring in, scoring goals will happen eventually. If you hammer defense, the worst you can do is tie 0-0. You can't let them score."

Domination

Jerry Yeagley ended his varsity career with a 544-101-45 record (.821 winning percentage). All thirty-one of his varsity years were winning seasons. He experi-

ten struggled and had to find a way to succeed. But even in the tough times, the Hoosiers knew they would get back on track within a few games. "Adversity never made this team sit back," Pat McGauley said. "It's consistency over thirty, forty years. It's so difficult to repeat and keep going back and being at the top. Everybody wants to beat you. Coach's ability to beat teams on a daily basis was amazing." The 2003 team had the worst start in IU history, at 2-3-4. But then the defense came together, and they ended up winning a sixth national championship. "You knew eventually they would find their chemistry and it would be a rock back there," Brian Plotkin said. "In practice we just worked really hard. Mistakes were happening. Then they weren't happening. And when they did, they were quick to correct it. They were all expecting more from each other."

In the close games, the Hoosiers never stopped fighting. If their defense could hold on to a one-goal lead, they had a good chance to win. "I don't know if we ever lost by more than three goals," Tom Redmond said. "Coach always believed that in tight games, defense would come through. In soccer there are so many 1-0 games. It really does boil down to defense when it comes down to crunch time." Caleb Porter agreed: "We like to attack and we like to defend, but we're going to make sure the defense is what holds us in games."

The Hoosiers knew how to dominate on their home turf, and their opponents often feared playing in Bloomington. "Stepping out on the field, we knew other teams were intimidated by Indiana," Pat Noonan said. "It doesn't matter who's on the field. Seeing the fear on their faces. It's a domination we've had since Coach started off in the club days. Teams never like to play us, especially at Armstrong Stadium." And with so many fans travel-

Jay Nolly and his back line led the Hoosiers to the 2003 NCAA College Cup. Photo: Paul Riley, IU Athletics.

ing with the Hoosiers across the country, every arena felt like home. "We make every field our home field," Jed Zayner said.

Desire, Passion, Competition

Jerry Yeagley was one of the most competitive men that most of his players had ever seen. The passion shone clearly in his eyes. He inspired his players with his desire for the game and his constant drive to excel. "You just wanted to win and work hard for the guy," Juergen Sommer said. "He was competitive and really wanted to win. It drove him crazy to lose. He was

John Swann, Ned Grabavoy, Danny O'Rourke, and Vijay Dias form a wall to stop an opponent's freekick attempt in the 2002 season. Photo: Paul Riley, IU Athletics.

very passionate about the game and people who played." His competitive drive didn't stop with soccer. Along the way he challenged many to a basketball game, a golf game, arm wrestling, or even Indian wrestling. "You won't find a more competitive person in anything you do with him or against him," John Trask said. "I remember him Indian wrestling and arm wrestling. You could see him locked up against a six-foot defender and not budging." And he rarely, if ever, lost.

Yeagley passed his competitive nature along to his children as well. "When my dad dropped me off at preschool, there was a ramp from the car up to the door," Todd said. "We used to have a little race every day. It just shows his competitive nature. And in many ways he was trying to instill that in me." His daughter caught the competitive bug, too. "It's sick how competitive we were as kids," Yvette said. "The first time I went home with Scott to Cleveland and met his family, we all decided to play an interactive game. Give me five minutes and I start barking orders. They looked at me and said, 'You are your father's daughter.'"

Former assistant coach Don Rawson said that it's only natural for Yeagley's kids to be so competitive. After all, they learned from the best. "He thrives on competition," Rawson said. "He absolutely loves the competitive arena. Not just the competition itself. He also enjoys the preparation for it. He's the kind of person that enjoys going to class and studying and taking the final exam. In soccer terms, he enjoys the preparation of training, executing the training, and playing the games."

As a player, Yeagley exhibited the same strong desire for defending that he would later ask of his players. As a member of his college team, he loved the opportunity to shut opponents down. On the field, Yeagley gave it his all. He never cheated. He never slacked off. As a coach, he expected his players to play with those same qualities. "You have to be a warrior," Yuri Lavrinenko said. "The way Yeags played, he was a tough defender, a tough player. That's what he expects out of everybody. You have to fight for 50/50 balls. You can't give up. That's something that was inbred in him, every player and every coach."

Jerry Yeagley ranks among the best of the best when it comes to coaching at the national level. "As I look at the history of IU at the collegiate level, we've had coaches that were the best in their sport: Doc Counsilman, Jerry Yeagley, Hobie Billingsley, Sam Bell, Bob Knight . . . We've been so lucky at IU to have great coaches," Athletic Director Terry Clapacs said. "Jerry brought great honor to the university and our department." Yeagley had a true passion for the game. He had a true desire to win. And he may have been the most competitive coach on the planet. He led his Hoosiers to the top of the polls around the country on a consistent basis, and he did it with class, a wink, and a smile. Defense won six national soccer championships for Indiana University, and Jerry Yeagley coached winners.

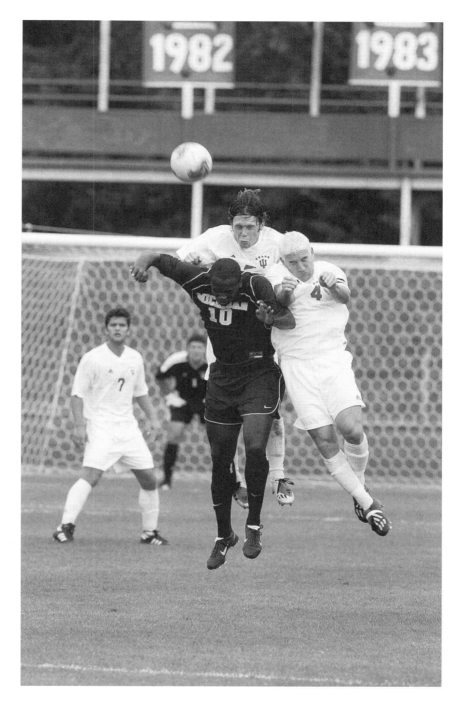

Danny O'Rourke and John Swann win the ball over an opponent during the 2002 season. The duo helped IU's defense earn eight shutouts that year. Photo: Paul Riley, IU Athletics.

STATISTICS AND PLAYERS

Hoosier Letterwinners

Ahumada, Matt	2000	Compani, Behatz	1973
Akman, Tanner	1973	Correia, Mike	1985–88
Alavanja, Lazo	1995–98	Coufal, Scott	1993–96
Ambersley, Mike	2001–02	Cowan, Todd	1994–95
Andert, Joseph	1976–79	Cox, Alex	2000
Anhaeuser, Michael	1988–91	Cox, Todd	1989
Archer, Joseph	1975–76	Coyer, Matt	1989–92
Atinay, Charles	1988–91	Crawford, George	1992–95
		Creager, Heath	2002
Baciu, Chris	1993	Crockford, Brian	1991–93
Badger, Greg	2001–03	Crockford, Jim	1987–90
Bannister, Jeff	1992–95		
Barber, Sasha	2000	Das, Biman	1984
Barg, Stephen	1976	Deering, Chad	1989–90
Barkett, Gus	1973–74	Deery, Simon	1995–98
Becker, David	1989	de St. Aubin, Bobby	2000–01
Behringer, Marc	1986–88	Desmuke, Daniel	1975
Berry, Tom	1990	Dias, Vijay	2000–03
Betancourt, Armando	1979–81	DiBernardo, Angelo	1976–78
Bobb, Robin	1973–74	DiBernardo, Paul	1981–84
Bock, Michael	1999–2002	Dieterle, Julian	2003
Boncek, Dave	1981–84	DiGuardi, Gino	1995–98
Bootes, Damon	1987–89	Doerr, Steve	1977–80
Bowditch, Michael	2001–02	Donaldson, Nick	2000
Bubalovic, Mirsad	1990–91		
Burks, Steve	1973–76	Eichinger, F. A.	1974
		Eise, David	1984–87
Calkins, Scott	1989–90	Ellsworth, Cliff	2001
Carlson, David	1986		
Carlson, Rob	1988–89	Fadeski, Dennis	1996–99
Carrascosa, Rolando	1995	Fajkus, Charlie	1975–78
Casaburo, Chris	1990–91, 1993	Fall, Ibrahima	1973
Casaburo, Tom	1987–89, 1991	Fauser, Christian	1981, 1983–85
Castro, Rodrigo	1983–86	Feld, Cary	1974–77
Cavallo, Joey	1995–96	Ferland, Thomas	1982
Cerroni, J. T.	1994–97	Fleck, Bill	1989–90
Cerroni, Tony	1996, 1998	Fortune, Hudson	1975–78
Chirico, Jordan	2002–03	Fortune, Mark	1977
Chorvat, Marcus	1999–2002	Freitag, Mike	1976–79
Christian, Lucas	2000	Fresen, Gary	1973–74
Clark, Mike	1991–94	Freud, David	1974–75
		Fundenberger, Matt	1997–2000

Gallagher, Peter	1982	Kelley, Joe	1975
Garcia, Nick	1997–99	Kennedy, Greg	1980–83
Gauvain, Dave	1985	Killough, Bruce	1984–87
Getman, Mike	1978, 1981	King, Dan	1981–84
Ginsberg, Craig	1991–94	King, Sean	1994
Glenn, Rudy	1976–79	Kirchner, Bob	1973–75
Godat, Ken	1986–87, 1989–90	Kirchner, Stephen	1975
Gold, Noah	2002	Klein, Chris	1994–97
Goldsmidt, Mark	1978–81	Kornhaber, Steve	1973–74
Goldstein, Eric	2002	Korol, Aleksey	1996–99
Gorrity, Manuel	1980, 1982–84	Kovalenko, Dema	1996–98
Grabavoy, Ned	2001–03	Kropp, Joe	1973–74
Grace, Dennis	1975	Kulenski, Nick	2003
Griggs, Brad	1997		
		Lavrinenko, Yuri	1996–99
Haller, Herb	1985–88	Lawrence, Don	1988
Hammer, Ryan	1998, 2000–01	Laxgang, Mark	1980–84
Hampton, Len	1981, 1983	Layman, Craig	1981–82
Hannig, T. J.	1997–2000	Layman, Lance	1982, 1984–85
Hardy, Tim	1992–95	Leon, Kenneth	1974
Harris, Tory	1995	Ley, Leo	1973
Haugen, Lars	1989–90	Leytze, Bob	1983
Hawley, Tyler	1998–2000	Lobring, Wane	1990–93
Hayden, John Michael	2003	Londergan, Ben	1995–97
Hocking, Randy	1977–78	Losh, Brian	1993–94
Hussey, Thomas	1974–76	Loyal, Michael	1974–75
Hylla, Mike	1981–84	Luciano, Andre	1991–92
Hylla, Tim	1983–86		
		McCarthy, Edward	1975
Isger, Matt	1987–90	McCartney, Michael	1982, 1984
Iung, Ernane	1981	McClements, Timothy	1984
Iung, Silvio	1982	McDevitt, Nick	2000
		McGauley, Pat	1979–81
Jambois, Stephen	1976	McGonagle, Timothy	1973–74
Jermack, Greg	1997	McGuire, Chris	1991
Johnson, B.	1986	Mack, Ryan	1998–2000, 2002
Johnson, John	1985–86	Maisonneuve, Brian	1991–94
Johnston, J. D.	2001	Margolin, Barry	1985–87
Jorgensen, Jason	1998	Martin, W. M.	1980
		Meek, Trey	2001, 2003
Kabanas, Steve	1980	Mercurio, James	1974–77
Kallay, Bob	1990	Merritt, Scott	1993–96
Kapsalis, Dan	1982–84	Meschbach, Robert	1977–80
Kapsalis, Dean	1989–90, 1992–93	Meyer, Keith	1980, 1982–84
Kapsalis, Paul	1984, 1986–87	Meyer, Steve	1979–82
Katner, Simon	1985–88	Mitrovich, Nick	1983–84
Katsinis, John	1974–75	Moor, Drew	2003
Kaull, Kevin	1981	Mukete, Abel	1973
Kean, Raymond	1974–77		
Keenan, Chris	1984–86	Nelson, Robert	1973
Keenan, Tommy	1995–98	Nolly, Jay	2001–03
Keller, Ray	1981	Noonan, Pat	1999–02
Keller, Steve	1991–94		

Oliver, Rudolpho	1981	Shelton, David	1974–77
Olson, Matthew	1986, 1988	Shinabarger, Drew	2000–02
O'Rourke, Danny	2001–03	Shinneman, J.	1985
Oswald, Chris	1980–83	Simanton, Mark	1976–79
		Simonsohn, Dan	1974
Paddock, Chris	1984–85	Sloane, Mike	1984–85
Parrish, Andrew	1995–98	Smith, Aaron	1985
Paul, John	1987–90	Snow, B. J.	1996–99
Peltonen, Craig	1978–79	Snow, Ken	1987–90
Perry, George	1975–77	Snow, Steve	1989
Peterson, Chris	1980–83	Sommer, Juergen	1987–90
Peterson, Jacob	2003	Spirk, Justin	2000
Peterson, Kevin	1977	Spray, Rick	1975–76
Phillips, Sean	1992–93	Stalter, Todd	1989–90
Plotkin, Brian	2002–03	Stewart, Derek	1984
Pohn, Jordan	1987	Stollmeyer, John	1982–85
Pomeroy, Chris	2001–03	Stoyanovich, Pete	1985–87
Popp, David	1996	Swann, John	1999–2002
Porter, Caleb	1994–97	Sweet, Mark	1986
Prall, David	2000–02		
Presser, Phil	1999–2002	Tauber, Brandon	1999
Priest, Wes	1987–88	Tauber, Justin	1997–2000
Putna, John	1976–79	Thompson, Gregg	1978, 1980–82
		Trask, John	1984–87
Rapp, Dana	1984	Trigg, Bob	1987
Rawson, Donald	1973–74	Tsandes, Ted	1988
Razumich, Jerry	1974	Tudela, Josh	2003
Redmond, Tom	1974–75		
Reiher, Josh	2001–02	VanBuskirk, John	1990–92, 1994
Reiswerg, Matt	2000–02	Veldman, Thomas	1973
Rife, Josh	2000–01	Vieira, Kim	1973–74
Riggs-Miller, Henry	1982		
Ripley, Eric	1996–98	Waldschmit, James	1974–75
Ripmaster, Austin	1998	Walsh, Timothy	1978–81
Robson, Kevin	2003	Walters, Timothy	1976–79
Rodgers, Blake	1990–93	Ward, Brandon	1991–94
Rodriguez, Esmundo	1995	Warren, Doug	1999
Roest, Han	1985–88	Weiss, Brad	1992
Rogers, Colin	1998–2001	Weiss, Harry	1992–95
Romanelli, Dominic	1984	Westbrook, Steve	1977–80
Rossiter, Chris	1984	Wicker, Roger	1979–81
Roy, Shashi	1979–80	Wilcox, Toby	1990–91
Rupprecht, Bryan	1992	Wilke, Steve	1976–77
Russell, Joel	1990–91	Wong, Peter	1973
		Wright, David	1991, 1993–95
Sagstetter, David	1976		
Schmid, Joe	1979–81, 1983	Yarborough, Ernie	1992–95
Schulenburg, John	1974–75	Yassin, Azmil	1973–74
Sciortino, Chris	1987–88	Yates, Pat	2002–03
Sendobry, Jeff	1978–79	Yeagley, Todd	1991–94
Shanker, Joel	1991–94		
Shapert, Sean	1986–89	Zarr, Joe	1997
		Zayner, Jed	2003
		Zubizerreta, Iker	1981–84

Club Records (1963-1972)

Overall Record: 78-25-7

IU	1963	Opp.
0	Ball State	0
5	Calvin	5
5	Dayton	3
2	Earlham	2
4	Illinois	1
3	Indiana Tech	1
0	Michigan State	7
4	Ohio State	2
4	Purdue	1
27		22

Record: 6-1-3

IU	1964	Opp.
4	Ball State	1
5	Calvin	2
5	Dayton	2
2	Earlham	1
9	Illinois	1
5	Indiana Tech	2
3	Michigan State	3
2	Ohio State	1
6	Purdue	1
2	St. Louis	8
43		22

Record: 8-1-1

IU	1965	Opp.
4	Ball State	1
2	E. Illinois	0
4	Ohio State	2
0	Michigan State	6
9	Notre Dame	1
5	Purdue	4
7	Illinois	1
3	Indiana Tech	1
9	Northwestern	0
5	Earlham	2
48		18

Record: 9-1

IU	1966	Opp.
6	Northwestern	0
2	St. Louis	2
2	E. Illinois	1
5	Depauw	0
1	Earlham	3
4	Ball State	2
6	Illinois	2
9	Indiana State	0
7	Notre Dame	2
3	Purdue	0
45		12

Record: 8-1-1

IU	1967	Opp.
4	Ball State	2
3	E. Illinois	1
3	Illinois	3
2	Depauw	1
0	Akron	1
3	Chicago Illini	2
1	Purdue	2
3	Goshen	2
0	Earlham	2
6	Northwestern	0
0	St. Louis	4
4	Notre Dame	2
29		22

Record: 7-4-1

IU	1968	Opp.
2	Goshen	1
6	Ball State	0
2	Illinios	1
7	S. Illinois	3
4	E. Illinois	1
5	Northwestern	0
0	Quincy	1
0	St. Louis	5
0	Earlham	1
4	Grace	1
2	Purdue	1
32		15

Record: 8-3

IU	1969	Opp.
1	Ohio University	1
1	SIU-Edwardsville	6
4	Depauw	1
0	SIU Carbondale	1
1	Chicago Illini	2
5	Purdue	2
1	Northwestern	0
10	Kentucky	1
0	E. Illinois	3
6	Illinois	1
3	Earlham	4
2	Ball State	0
34		22

Record: 6-5-1

IU	1970	Opp.
2	Illinois	3
3	Depauw	4
1	Purdue	2
0	Chicago Illini	3
2	Indiana Tech	1
1	SIU Carbondale	2
2	Notre Dame	0
0	E. Illinois	4
0	St. Louis	8
3	Ball State	1
0	Earlham	5
14		33

Record: 3-8

IU	1971	Opp.
3	Notre Dame	0
7	Kentucky	0
5	Depauw	0
5	Purdue	0
3	Illinois	1
13	Indiana Tech	1
7	Ohio State	1
5	Marion	1
1	E. Illinois	0
4	Wabash	1
4	Ball State	0
3	Earlham	1
60		6

Record: 12-0

IU	1972	Opp.
4	Notre Dame	0
5	Illinois	0
6	Kentucky	0
6	Ball State	2
6	Cincinnati	1
4	Depauw	1
2	Marion	1
2	Eastern Illinois	3
3	Purdue	1
1	Cleveland State	0
5	Earlham	2
3	Ohio State	1
47		12

Record: 11-1

Varsity Records (1973-2003)

1973   Record: 12-2

Date	Opponent	W/L/T	Score	Record
Sept. 14	at Notre Dame	W	5-1	1-0
Sept. 22	Goshen	W	7-1	2-0
Sept. 25	at Wabash	W	3-1	3-0
Sept. 28	Kentucky	W	5-0	4-0
Oct. 3	at Ball State	W	2-0	5-0
Oct. 6	Indiana State	W	10-0	6-0
Oct. 12	at Cincinnati	W	8-2	7-0
Oct. 17	DePauw	W	4-0	8-0
Oct. 20	at Ohio State	W	6-0	9-0
Oct. 24	at Eastern Illinois	L	0-1	9-1
Oct. 26	at Purdue	W	6-0	10-1
Nov. 3	at Cleveland State	L	0-1	10-2
Nov. 7	Earlham	W	5-0	11-2
Nov. 9	Marion	W	7-0	12-2

1974   Record: 14-3

Date	Opponent	W/L/T	Score	Record
Sept. 13	Notre Dame	W	11-1	1-0
Sept. 21	Dayton	W	7-0	2-0
Sept. 23	at Goshen	W	2-0	3-0
Sept. 27	Purdue[1]	W	7-1	4-0
Sept. 28	Ball State[1]	W	3-0	5-0
Oct. 2	Wabash	W	2-0	6-0
Oct. 4	Michigan	W	10-1	7-0
Oct. 11	Cincinnati	W	7-0	8-0
Oct. 16	at DePauw	W	6-0	9-0
Oct. 18	at Kentucky	W	2-1	10-0
Oct. 22	Eastern Illinois	L	1-2	10-1
Oct. 24	MacMurray[2]	W	4-1	11-1
Oct. 25	at Illinois-Chicago[2]	W	2-1	12-1
Nov. 3	Cleveland State	L	1-2	12-2
Nov. 5	at Earlham	W	5-0	13-2
Nov. 8	Michigan State	W	3-0	14-2

NCAA Tournament

Date	Opponent	W/L/T	Score	Record
Nov. 16	at SIU-Edwardsville	L	0-2	14-3

[1]State Tournament (Bloomington)
[2]Ill.-Chicago Tournament (Chicago)

1975   Record: 13-3-1

Date	Opponent	W/L/T	Score	Record
Sept. 12	at Cincinnati	W	5-2	1-0
Sept. 17	at Wabash	W	9-0	2-0

Date	Opponent	W/L/T	Score	Record
Sept. 20	at Dayton	W	4-0	3-0
Sept. 24	Goshen	W	6-2	4-0
Sept. 26	Purdue[1]	W	3-0	5-0
Sept. 27	Ball State[1]	W	4-0	6-0
Oct. 4	at Akron	L	1-2	6-1
Oct. 5	Western Illinois	W	2-1	7-1
Oct. 11	at St. Louis	L	1-4	7-2
Oct. 15	DePauw	W	9-0	8-2
Oct. 18	Wisconsin[2]	W	5-0	9-2
Oct. 19	Michigan State[2]	W	6-0	10-2
Oct. 22	at Eastern Illinois (OT)	T	1-1	10-2-1
Oct. 25	Illinois-Chicago	W	3-1	11-2-1
Nov. 1	Cleveland State	L	1-2	11-3-1
Nov. 5	Earlham	W	8-0	12-3-1
Nov. 7	Kentucky	W	11-0	13-3-1

[1]State Tournament (Bloomington)
[2]Big Ten Classic (Columbus, Ohio)

1976   Record: 18-1-1

Date	Opponent	W/L/T	Score	Record
Sept. 15	UW-Milwaukee	W	6-0	1-0
Sept. 17	at Western Illinois (OT)	T	0-0	1-0-1
Sept. 19	Dayton	W	6-0	2-0-1
Sept. 24	Ball State[1]	W	6-0	3-0-1
Sept. 25	Indiana State[1]	W	19-0	4-0-1
Oct. 2	at Akron (OT)	W	3-2	5-0-1
Oct. 10	St. Louis	W	5-1	6-0-1
Oct. 13	Cincinnati	W	7-0	7-0-1
Oct. 16	Wisconsin[2]	W	2-1	8-0-1
Oct. 17	Ohio State[2]	W	4-2	9-0-1
Oct. 20	Eastern Illinois	W	1-0	10-0-1
Oct. 23	at Wheaton[3]	W	2-1	11-0-1
Oct. 24	Northern Illinois[3]	W	3-1	12-0-1
Oct. 31	Cleveland State	W	5-0	13-0-1
Nov. 3	at Earlham	W	13-0	14-0-1
Nov. 5	at Kentucky	W	7-0	15-0-1

NCAA Tournament

Date	Opponent	W/L/T	Score	Record
Nov. 21	Akron	W	2-1	16-0-1
Nov. 28	SIU-Edwardsville	W	1-0	17-0-1

NCAA College Cup (Philadelphia)

Date	Opponent	W/L/T	Score	Record
Dec. 5	Hartwick	W	2-1	18-0-1
Dec. 7	San Francisco	L	0-1	18-1-1

[1]State Tournament (West Lafayette)
[2]Big Ten Classic (East Lansing, Mich.)
[3]Wheaton Classic (Wheaton, Ill.)

1977   *Record: 12-2-1*

Date	Opponent	W/L/T	Score	Record
Sept. 10	at UW-Milwaukee	W	2-1	1-0
Sept. 14	Wheaton	W	6-0	2-0
Sept. 18	at Dayton	W	9-0	3-0
Sept. 25	San Francisco (OT)	T	1-1	3-0-1
Oct. 2	at Akron	W	5-0	4-0-1
Oct. 12	at Cincinnati	W	1-0	5-0-1
Oct. 14	Michigan State[1]	W	7-0	6-0-1
Oct. 15	Wisconsin[1]	W	8-1	7-0-1
Oct. 19	at Eastern Illinois	W	1-0	8-0-1
Oct. 21	at Illinois-Chicago[2]	W	2-0	9-0-1
Oct. 29	at Cleveland State	L	0-2	9-1-1
Nov. 2	Ball State	W	11-1	10-1-1
Nov. 6	Purdue	W	7-0	11-1-1
Nov. 12	at St. Louis	W	1-0	12-1-1

NCAA Tournament

Nov. 17	at SIU-Edwardsville	L	2-3	12-2-1

[1]Big Ten Classic (Bloomington)
[2]Illinois-Chicago Tournament (Chicago)

1978   *Record: 23-2*

Date	Opponent	W/L/T	Score	Record
Sept. 3	UCLA	W	2-1	1-0
Sept. 7	at Rhode Island	W	2-0	2-0
Sept. 9	at Connecticut	W	4-2	3-0
Sept. 11	at Springfield	W	4-0	4-0
Sept. 16	Penn State[1]	W	2-0	5-0
Sept. 17	Hartwick[1]	W	4-0	6-0
Sept. 22	at San Jose State[2]	W	1-0	7-0
Sept. 23	San Francisco[2]	W	2-1	8-0
Sept. 30	at Akron	W	2-1	9-0
Oct. 8	St. Louis	W	2-0	10-0
Oct. 11	Cincinnati	W	6-2	11-0
Oct. 14	Ohio State[3]	W	2-0	12-0
Oct. 15	at Wisconsin[3]	W	6-0	13-0
Oct. 18	Eastern Illinois	W	2-0	14-0
Oct. 20	at Evansville	W	1-0	15-0
Oct. 22	Notre Dame	W	7-1	16-0
Oct. 29	Cleveland State	L	0-1	16-1
Nov. 1	at Ball State	W	6-2	17-1
Nov. 5	Dayton	W	5-0	18-1
Nov. 8	at Purdue	W	8-0	19-1
Nov. 12	UW-Milwaukee	W	2-1	20-1

NCAA Tournament

| Nov. 19 | Cleveland State | W | 3-1 | 21-1 |
| Nov. 26 | SIU-Edwardsville | W | 2-0 | 22-1 |

NCAA College Cup (Tampa, Fla.)

| Dec. 6 | Philadelphia Textile | W | 2-0 | 23-1 |
| Dec. 8 | San Francisco | L[4] | 0-2 | 23-2 |

[1]Big Red Classic (Bloomington)
[2]Shriners Classic (San Jose, Calif.)
[3]Big Ten Classic (Madison, Wis.)
[4]Title was later vacated

1979   Record: 19-2-2

Date	Opponent	W/L/T	Score	Record
Sept. 1	UW-Green Bay[1]	W	5-0	1-0
Sept. 2	at UW-Milwaukee[1]	W	2-0	2-0
Sept. 9	Purdue	W	5-0	3-0
Sept. 15	Southern Methodist[2]	L	0-1	3-1
Sept. 16	Appalachian State[2]	W	3-0	4-1
Sept. 21	North Texas State[3]	W	6-0	5-1
Sept. 22	Rockhurst[3]	W	2-0	6-1
Sept. 28	at Notre Dame	W	4-0	7-1
Sept. 30	Akron	W	3-0	8-1
Oct. 5	at St. Louis	W	3-1	9-1
Oct. 10	at Cincinnati	W	6-0	10-1
Oct. 13	Illinois[4]	W	5-0	11-1
Oct. 14	Michigan State[4]	W	5-0	12-1
Oct. 17	at Eastern Illinois (OT)	T	1-1	12-1-1
Oct. 19	South Carolina[5]	W	1-0	13-1-1
Oct. 20	Evansville[5]	W	1-0	14-1-1
Oct. 28	at Cleveland State (OT)	T	1-1	14-1-2
Oct. 31	Ball State	W	13-0	15-1-2
Nov. 4	Evansville	W	4-0	16-1-2
Nov. 9	at Dayton	W	7-0	17-1-2
Nov. 11	at Minnesota	W	6-0	18-1-2

NCAA Tournament

| Nov. 18 | Cleveland State | W | 5-0 | 19-1-2 |
| Nov. 25 | at Penn State | L | 0-2 | 19-2-2 |

[1]UW-Milwaukee Kickoff Classic
[2]Big Red Classic (Bloomington)
[3]SIU Classic (Edwardsville, Ill.)
[4]Big Ten Classic (Bloomington)
[5]Wheaton Classic (Wheaton, Ill.)

1980   Record: 22-3-1

Date	Opponent	W/L/T	Score	Record
Sept. 1	at SMU (OT)	T	1-1	0-0-1
Sept. 2	at North Texas	L	0-1	0-1-1
Sept. 7	Connecticut	W	1-0	1-1-1
Sept. 11	at Purdue	W	10-0	2-1-1
Sept. 14	Penn State	W	2-0	3-1-1
Sept. 19	Portland[1]	W	4-2	4-1-1
Sept. 20	at SIU-Edwardsville[1]	W	1-0	5-1-1
Sept. 24	Western Michigan	W	4-0	6-1-1
Sept. 27	at Akron	W	3-1	7-1-1
Sept. 28	Notre Dame	W	4-0	8-1-1
Oct. 5	St. Louis	L	0-3	8-2-1
Oct. 8	Cincinnati	W	9-0	9-2-1
Oct. 11	Michigan State[2]	W	5-0	10-2-1
Oct. 12	at Ohio State[2]	W	2-0	11-2-1
Oct. 15	Eastern Illinois	W	1-0	12-2-1
Oct. 19	UW-Milwaukee	W	3-0	13-2-1
Oct. 26	Cleveland State	W	1-0	14-2-1
Oct. 29	at Ball State	W	4-1	15-2-1
Nov. 2	at Evansville	W	3-2	16-2-1
Nov. 3	at Southern Indiana	W	1-0	17-2-1
Nov. 7	Dayton	W	6-0	18-2-1
Nov. 9	at Wisconsin[3]	W	2-0	19-2-1

NCAA Tournament

Date	Opponent	W/L/T	Score	Record
Nov. 30	Cleveland State	W	3-0	20-2-1
Dec. 7	Penn State	W	3-1	21-2-1

NCAA College Cup (Tampa, Fla.)

Date	Opponent	W/L/T	Score	Record
Dec. 13	Hartwick	W	5-0	22-2-1
Dec. 15	San Francisco	L	3-4	22-3-1

[1]SIU Classic (Edwardsville, Ill.)
[2]Big Ten Classic (Columbus, Ohio)
[3]Big Ten Title Match (Madison, Wis.)

1981   Record: 20-3

Date	Opponent	W/L/T	Score	Record
Sept. 2	at Vermont	W	2-0	1-0
Sept. 4	at Boston College	W	1-0	2-0
Sept. 6	at Connecticut	L	1-3	2-1
Sept. 13	San Francisco (OT)	W	2-1	3-1
Sept. 20	Akron	W	3-1	4-1
Sept. 22	Purdue	W	6-0	5-1
Sept. 27	SIU-Edwardsville	W	3-2	6-1
Oct. 2	at St. Louis	L	0-1	6-2
Oct. 4	Louisville	W	6-1	7-2
Oct. 7	Southern Indiana	W	7-1	8-2

Date	Opponent	W/L/T	Score	Record
Oct. 10	Illinois[1]	W	8-0	9-2
Oct. 11	Michigan State[1]	W	5-1	10-2
Oct. 14	at Bowling Green	W	7-1	11-2
Oct. 17	at UW-Milwaukee	W	1-0	12-2
Oct. 18	at Marquette	W	2-0	13-2
Oct. 24	at Cleveland State	W	6-0	14-2
Oct. 25	at Notre Dame	W	2-0	15-2
Oct. 28	Ball State	W	7-1	16-2
Nov. 1	Evansville	W	4-0	17-2
Nov. 6	at Dayton	W	4-0	18-2
Nov. 8	Wisconsin[2]	W	1-0	19-2

NCAA Tournament

Date	Opponent	W/L/T	Score	Record
Nov. 22	Wisconsin	W	5-1	20-2
Nov. 29	at Philadelphia Textile	L	0-1	20-3

[1]Big Ten Classic (Bloomington)
[2]Big Ten Title Match (Bloomington)

1982   Record: 21-3-1

Date	Opponent	W/L/T	Score	Record
Sept. 4	Alabama A&M (OT)	L	1-2	0-1
Sept. 10	Marquette	W	4-0	1-1
Sept. 15	at Fresno State (OT)	L	1-2	1-2
Sept. 17	at San Francisco (OT)	L	2-3	1-3
Sept. 19	at Stanford	W	4-2	2-3
Sept. 22	at SIU-Edwardsville	W	1-0	3-3
Sept. 24	Notre Dame	W	4-0	4-3
Sept. 29	Kentucky	W	8-0	5-3
Oct. 2	St. Louis	W	4-0	6-3
Oct. 6	Purdue	W	4-0	7-3
Oct. 8	at Akron	W	2-1	8-3
Oct. 9	Ohio State[1]	W	1-0	9-3
Oct. 10	at Michigan State[1]	W	7-0	10-3
Oct. 13	Bowling Green	W	1-0	11-3
Oct. 16	UW-Milwaukee	W	3-0	12-3
Oct. 22	Cleveland State	W	3-0	13-3
Oct. 27	at Louisville	W	3-1	14-3
Oct. 31	at Evansville (OT)	T	1-1	14-3-1
Nov. 1	at Southern Indiana	W	1-0	15-3-1
Nov. 5	Dayton	W	3-0	16-3-1
Nov. 7	at Wisconsin[2] (OT)	W	2-1	17-3-1

NCAA Tournament

Date	Opponent	W/L/T	Score	Record
Nov. 21	Evansville	W	1-0	18-3-1
Nov. 28	Philadelphia Textile	W	2-0	19-3-1
Dec. 5	SIU-Edwardsville	W	1-0	20-3-1

NCAA Finals (Ft. Lauderdale, Fla.)

Date	Opponent	W/L/T	Score	Record
Dec. 11	Duke (8OT)	W	2-1	21-3-1

[1]Big Ten Classic (East Lansing, Mich.)
[2]Big Ten Title Match (Madison, Wis.)

1983   Record: 21-1-4

Date	Opponent	W/L/T	Score	Record
Sept. 2	at Penn State (OT)	L	1-2	0-1
Sept. 4	at George Mason	W	2-1	1-1
Sept. 9	SIU-Edwardsville	W	2-0	2-1
Sept. 11	at Kentucky	W	4-1	3-1
Sept. 16	Duke[1] (OT)	T	0-0	3-1-1
Sept. 17	San Francisco[1]	W	3-0	4-1-1
Sept. 23	Northwestern	W	11-0	5-1-1
Sept. 25	at Notre Dame	W	4-0	6-1-1
Sept. 28	Purdue	W	8-0	7-1-1
Sept. 30	at St. Louis (OT)	T	2-2	7-1-2
Oct. 2	Ohio State	W	3-2	8-1-2
Oct. 7	Akron (OT)	T	0-0	8-1-3
Oct. 12	at Bowling Green (OT)	W	2-1	9-1-3
Oct. 16	at UW-Milwaukee	W	1-0	10-1-3
Oct. 22	at Cleveland State	W	3-0	11-1-3
Oct. 26	Louisville	W	14-0	12-1-3
Oct. 30	Evansville (OT)	W	2-1	13-1-3
Nov. 3	at Dayton	W	5-0	14-1-3
Nov. 5	Michigan State[2]	W	4-2	15-1-3
Nov. 6	at Ohio State[2]	W	4-1	16-1-3
Nov. 9	at Alabama A&M (OT)	T	1-1	16-1-4
Nov. 13	at Wisconsin[3]	W	4-0	17-1-4

NCAA Tournament

Date	Opponent	W/L/T	Score	Record
Nov. 20	Akron (OT)	W	2-1	18-1-4
Nov. 27	St. Louis	W	2-1	19-1-4
Dec. 4	Virginia	W	3-1	20-1-4

NCAA Finals (Ft. Lauderdale, Fla.)

Date	Opponent	W/L/T	Score	Record
Dec. 10	Columbia (OT)	W	1-0	21-1-4

[1]adidas-MetLife Classic (Bloomington)
[2]Big Ten Eastern Tournament (Columbus, Ohio)
[3]Big Ten Title Match (Madison, Wis.)

1984   Record: 22-2-2

Date	Opponent	W/L/T	Score	Record
Sept. 1	San Diego State[1]	W	2-1	1-0
Sept. 2	at UNLV[1]	W	3-2	2-0
Sept. 8	Virginia[2]	W	1-0	3-0
Sept. 9	Clemson[2] (OT)	W	4-3	4-0
Sept. 14	California[3]	W	2-1	5-0
Sept. 15	at San Francisco[3]	W	1-0	6-0
Sept. 21	at Northwestern	W	5-0	7-0
Sept. 23	Notre Dame	W	5-1	8-0
Sept. 28	St. Louis (OT)	T	2-2	8-0-1
Sept. 30	at Ohio State (OT)	W	3-2	9-0-1
Oct. 3	Bowling Green	W	2-0	10-0-1
Oct. 6	Akron	W	3-1	11-0-1
Oct. 12	UW-Green Bay	W	4-2	12-0-1
Oct. 14	UW-Milwaukee	W	6-0	13-0-1
Oct. 21	Cleveland State	W	1-0	14-0-1
Oct. 28	at Evansville	W	4-3	15-0-1
Oct. 30	at SIU-Edwardsville	W	1-0	16-0-1
Nov. 3	Purdue[4]	W	4-1	17-0-1
Nov. 4	Michigan State[4]	W	2-0	18-0-1
Nov. 7	at Wisconsin[5] (OT)	T	0-0	18-0-2
Nov. 9	at Tampa[6]	W	3-1	19-0-2
Nov. 11	South Florida[6]	L	1-3	19-1-2

NCAA Tournament

Date	Opponent	W/L/T	Score	Record
Nov. 25	Evansville	W	5-0	20-1-2
Dec. 2	St. Louis	W	4-2	21-1-2
Dec. 9	Hartwick	W	2-1	22-1-2

NCAA Finals (Seattle, Wash.)

Date	Opponent	W/L/T	Score	Record
Dec. 16	Clemson	L	1-2	22-2-2

[1]Rebel Classic (Las Vegas, Nev.)
[2]adidas-MetLife Classic (Bloomington)
[3]MetLife Classic (San Francisco)
[4]Big Ten Eastern Tournament (Bloomington)
[5]Big Ten Title Match (Madison, Wis.)
[6]Tampa Classic (Tampa, Fla.)

1985   Record: 12-9-1

Date	Opponent	W/L/T	Score	Record
Sept. 1	at Hartford	W	5-0	1-0
Sept. 6	Clemson[1]	L	2-3	1-1
Sept. 7	UCLA[1]	L	0-1	1-2
Sept. 13	North Carolina State[2]	L	2-3	1-3
Sept. 15	at Duke[2]	L	0-2	1-4
Sept. 20	Ohio State	W	4-0	2-4
Sept. 22	at Notre Dame	W	4-0	3-4

Date	Opponent	W/L/T	Score	Record
Sept. 25	Purdue	W	8-1	4-4
Sept. 27	at St. Louis	L	1-2	4-5
Sept. 29	SIU-Edwardsville	W	3-2	5-5
Oct. 4	Akron	W	3-0	6-5
Oct. 9	at Bowling Green (OT)	T	3-3	6-5-1
Oct. 11	at UW-Green Bay	W	2-0	7-5-1
Oct. 13	at UW-Milwaukee	W	3-0	8-5-1
Oct. 18	at Cleveland State	W	2-1	9-5-1
Oct. 20	Marquette	W	2-1	10-5-1
Oct. 27	Evansville	L	0-3	10-6-1
Nov. 3	Michigan State	W	4-0	11-6-1
Nov. 9	at Florida International[3]	L	1-2	11-7-1
Nov. 10	Fresno State[3]	L	0-1	11-8-1

NCAA Tournament

Date	Opponent	W/L/T	Score	Record
Nov. 16	Akron	W	2-0	12-8-1
Nov. 24	at Evansville	L	0-3	12-9-1

[1]adidas-MetLife Classic (Bloomington)

[2]Duke Classic (Durham, N.C.)

[3]McDonald's Classic (Ft. Lauderdale, Fla.)

1986   Record: 9-6-4

Date	Opponent	W/L/T	Score	Record
Sept. 5	South Carolina[1]	L	1-2	0-1
Sept. 6	Virginia[1] (OT)	T	1-1	0-1-1
Sept. 12	Notre Dame	W	2-0	1-1-1
Sept. 14	at Michigan State	W	3-1	2-1-1
Sept. 19	Bowling Green	W	2-0	3-1-1
Sept. 21	at Ohio State	W	2-0	4-1-1
Sept. 24	Cincinnati	W	5-0	5-1-1
Sept. 28	St. Louis	L	1-3	5-2-1
Oct. 1	Miami (Ohio)	W	5-0	6-2-1
Oct. 5	at Akron	L	0-1	6-3-1
Oct. 10	UW-Green Bay	W	3-2	7-3-1
Oct. 12	UW-Milwaukee	W	2-0	8-3-1
Oct. 17	Cleveland State	W	2-0	9-3-1
Oct. 19	at Marquette (OT)	T	2-2	9-3-2
Oct. 24	at Clemson[2]	L	1-3	9-4-2
Oct. 26	American[2] (OT)	T	1-1	9-4-3
Nov. 2	at Evansville (OT)	T	1-1	9-4-4
Nov. 7	Florida International[3]	L	1-3	9-5-4
Nov. 9	at Tampa[3]	L	1-2	9-6-4

[1]adidas-MetLife Classic (Bloomington)

[2]Clemson-Umbro Invite (Clemson, S.C.)

[3]Tampa Classic (Tampa, Fla.)

1987   Record: 18-3

Date	Opponent	W/L/T	Score	Record
Sept. 4	South Carolina[1]	L	1-3	0-1
Sept. 5	Southern Methodist[1]	W	2-1	1-1
Sept. 11	Michigan State	W	6-0	2-1
Sept. 13	at Notre Dame (OT)	L	3-4	2-2
Sept. 16	Memphis State	W	3-1	3-2
Sept. 18	Ohio State	W	5-0	4-2
Sept. 20	at Bowling Green	W	3-1	5-2
Sept. 25	Akron	W	1-0	6-2
Sept. 27	at St. Louis	W	3-1	7-2
Sept. 30	Miami (Ohio)	W	8-0	8-2
Oct. 3	Seton Hall[2] (OT)	W	3-2	9-2
Oct. 4	Wake Forest[2]	W	4-0	10-2
Oct. 7	Northwestern	W	7-0	11-2
Oct. 9	Marquette	W	7-0	12-2
Oct. 16	at Cleveland State	W	6-2	13-2
Oct. 18	SIU-Edwardsville	W	3-0	14-2
Oct. 25	Evansville	W	1-0	15-2
Oct. 31	San Diego State[3]	W	3-2	16-2
Nov. 1	at UCLA[3]	W	2-1	17-2
Nov. 8	Wisconsin	W	2-0	18-2

NCAA Tournament

Date	Opponent	W/L/T	Score	Record
Nov. 22	Clemson	L	1-2	18-3

[1]adidas-MetLife Classic (Bloomington)
[2]Kenny Kent/Aces Classic (Evansville)
[3]UCLA-MetLife Classic (Westwood, Calif.)

1988   Record: 19-3-3

Date	Opponent	W/L/T	Score	Record
Sept. 2	North Carolina[1]	W	2-0	1-0
Sept. 3	UCLA[1]	W	2-1	2-0
Sept. 9	Notre Dame (OT)	T	1-1	2-0-1
Sept. 11	at Michigan State	W	6-0	3-0-1
Sept. 14	Northern Illinois	W	2-1	4-0-1
Sept. 16	Bowling Green	W	3-0	5-0-1
Sept. 18	at Ohio State	W	2-1	6-0-1
Sept. 23	Akron	W	3-1	7-0-1
Sept. 25	St. Louis	W	3-0	8-0-1
Sept. 27	Miami (Ohio)	W	6-0	9-0-1
Sept. 30	Santa Clara[2] (OT)	L	1-2	9-1-1
Oct. 1	George Washington[2]	L	0-1	9-2-1
Oct. 6	at Northwestern	W	3-0	10-2-1
Oct. 8	at Marquette	W	1-0	11-2-1
Oct. 9	UW-Milwaukee (OT)	W	2-1	12-2-1
Oct. 14	Cleveland State	W	5-0	13-2-1
Oct. 16	at SIU-Edwardsville	W	1-0	14-2-1

Date	Opponent	W/L/T	Score	Record
Oct. 29	at Evansville	L	0-1	14-3-1
Oct. 30	Wisconsin	W	2-0	15-3-1
Nov. 4	Stanford[3] (OT)	T	0-0	15-3-2
Nov. 6	at South Carolina[3] (OT)	T	1-1	15-3-3

NCAA Tournament

Nov. 20	Boston University	W	3-1	16-3-3
Nov. 27	Seton Hall	W	3-1	17-3-3

NCAA College Cup (Bloomington, Ind.)

Dec. 3	Portland	W	1-0	18-3-3
Dec. 4	Howard	W	1-0	19-3-3

[1]adidas-MetLife Classic (Bloomington)
[2]Kenny Kent/Aces Classic (Evansville)
[3]Carolina-MetLife Classic (Columbia, S.C.)

1989   Record: 18-2-2

Date	Opponent	W/L/T	Score	Record
Sept. 2	Virginia[1]	L	0-1	0-1
Sept. 3	St. Louis[1] (OT)	T	1-1	0-1-1
Sept. 9	Stanford[2]	W	1-0	1-1-1
Sept. 10	at San Francisco[2]	W	2-0	2-1-1
Sept. 13	Northern Illinois	W	1-0	3-1-1
Sept. 15	Ohio State	W	4-2	4-1-1
Sept. 17	at Bowling Green	W	2-1	5-1-1
Sept. 24	Harvard	W	7-2	6-1-1
Sept. 29	at Notre Dame	W	3-1	7-1-1
Oct. 1	Michigan State	W	3-0	8-1-1
Oct. 6	Marquette	W	3-1	9-1-1
Oct. 8	UW-Milwaukee	W	3-1	10-1-1
Oct. 13	Cincinnati	W	4-1	11-1-1
Oct. 15	SIU-Edwardsville	W	5-1	12-1-1
Oct. 18	Miami (Ohio)	W	8-0	13-1-1
Oct. 22	at Wisconsin (OT)	T	1-1	13-1-2
Oct. 29	Evansville	W	4-0	14-1-2
Nov. 3	George Mason[3]	W	2-1	15-1-2
Nov. 4	at Florida International[3]	W	7-0	16-1-2

NCAA Tournament

Nov. 18	George Washington	W	4-0	17-1-2
Nov. 26	Howard	W	1-0	18-1-2

NCAA College Cup (Piscataway, N.J.)

Dec. 2	Santa Clara	L	2-4	18-2-2

[1]adidas-MetLife Classic (Bloomington)
[2]adidas-MetLife Classic (San Francisco)
[3]Southern Bell Classic (Ft. Lauderdale, Fla.)

1990 Record: 16-4-2

Date	Opponent	W/L/T	Score	Record
Sept. 1	UCLA[1]	L	0-3	0-1
Sept. 2	at UNLV[1]	L	0-2	0-2
Sept. 7	San Francisco[2] (OT)	T	2-2	0-2-1
Sept. 8	Virginia[2]	W	2-1	1-2-1
Sept. 14	Bowling Green	W	4-1	2-2-1
Sept. 16	at Ohio State	W	4-0	3-2-1
Sept. 21	Akron (OT)	W	2-0	4-2-1
Sept. 23	at St. Louis	W	2-1	5-2-1
Sept. 30	at Michigan State (OT)	W	2-1	6-2-1
Oct. 3	Cincinnati	W	3-1	7-2-1
Oct. 6	at Marquette	W	2-1	8-2-1
Oct. 7	at UW-Milwaukee	W	2-1	9-2-1
Oct. 12	at Cleveland State	W	2-1	10-2-1
Oct. 14	Miami (Ohio)	W	4-0	11-2-1
Oct. 17	at Northern Illinois (OT)	T	1-1	11-2-2
Oct. 19	Northwestern	W	3-1	12-2-2
Oct. 21	Wisconsin (OT)	W	1-0	13-2-2
Oct. 27	Penn State[3]	W	2-1	14-2-2
Oct. 28	at South Carolina[3]	L	1-2	14-3-2

NCAA Tournament

Date	Opponent	W/L/T	Score	Record
Nov. 10	UW-Milwaukee	W	5-1	15-3-2
Nov. 17	St. Louis	W	2-1	16-3-2
Nov. 25	at Evansville	L	0-1	16-4-2

[1]UNLV Classic (Las Vegas, Nev.)
[2]adidas-MetLife Classic (Bloomington)
[3]MetLife Soccer Classic (Columbia, S.C.)

1991 Record: 19-3-2

Date	Opponent	W/L/T	Score	Record
Aug. 30	at Butler	W	5-0	1-0
Sept. 1	at Louisville	W	3-0	2-0
Sept. 6	Stanford[1] (OT)	T	2-2	2-0-1
Sept. 8	Penn State[1]	W	5-3	3-0-1
Sept. 13	Cleveland State	W	4-1	4-0-1
Sept. 15	Ohio State	W	5-0	5-0-1
Sept. 20	at Akron	W	1-0	6-0-1
Sept. 22	St. Louis	W	2-1	7-0-1
Sept. 27	at Notre Dame (OT)	W	4-1	8-0-1
Sept. 29	Michigan State	W	4-0	9-0-1
Oct. 5	Quincy[2] (OT)	T	0-0	9-0-2
Oct. 11	UW-Milwaukee	W	2-1	10-0-2
Oct. 13	at Bowling Green	W	2-0	11-0-2
Oct. 18	at Northwestern	W	8-0	12-0-2
Oct. 20	at Wisconsin	L	0-1	12-1-2

Date	Opponent	W/L/T	Score	Record
Oct. 25	Illinois State (OT)	W	3-0	13-1-2
Oct. 27	Marquette	W	4-2	14-1-2
Nov. 1	at Yale	L	1-2	14-2-2
Nov. 3	at Harvard	W	4-0	15-2-2

Big Ten Tournament (Bloomington)

Nov. 9	Penn State	W	4-2	16-2-2
Nov. 10	Wisconsin (OT)	W	2-0	17-2-2

NCAA Tournament

Nov. 24	Wisconsin	W	2-0	18-2-2
Dec. 1	SMU (OT; PKs)	W	3-2	19-2-2

NCAA College Cup (Tampa, Fla.)

Dec. 6	Santa Clara	L	0-2	19-3-2

[1]adidas-MetLife Classic (Bloomington)
[2]St. Louis Classic (St. Louis, Mo.)

1992   *Record: 14-6-4*

Date	Opponent	W/L/T	Score	Record
Sept. 5	Duke[1]	L	0-1	0-1
Sept. 6	UCLA[1]	L	0-1	0-2
Sept. 10	at Butler	W	3-0	1-2
Sept. 13	Kentucky	W	6-0	2-2
Sept. 18	Akron	W	1-0	3-2
Sept. 20	at St. Louis	L	0-2	3-3
Sept. 25	Notre Dame	W	3-0	4-3
Sept. 30	Louisville	W	4-1	5-3
Sept. 27	at Michigan State	W	3-0	6-3
Oct. 2	at Penn State (OT)	L	1-3	6-4
Oct. 9	at UW-Milwaukee (OT)	T	1-1	6-4-1
Oct. 11	Bowling Green	L	1-2	6-5-1
Oct. 16	Wisconsin (OT)	T	0-0	6-5-2
Oct. 18	Northwestern	W	8-0	7-5-2
Oct. 20	at Evansville	W	1-0	8-5-2
Oct. 23	Illinois State	W	1-0	9-5-2
Oct. 25	at Ohio State	W	4-1	10-5-2
Oct. 30	San Francisco[2] (OT)	T	1-1	10-5-3
Nov. 1	at Florida International[2] (OT)	T	0-0	10-5-4

Big Ten Tournament (Bloomington)

Nov. 7	Ohio State	W	1-0	11-5-4
Nov. 8	Penn State	W	2-1	12-5-4

NCAA Tournament

Date	Opponent	W/L/T	Score	Record
Nov. 15	at Evansville	W	4-1	13-5-4
Nov. 22	Washington	W	2-0	14-5-4
Nov. 29	at San Diego	L	0-2	14-6-4

[1]adidas-MetLife Classic (Bloomington)
[2]Florida International Classic (Ft. Lauderdale, Fla.)

1993   Record: 17-3-1

Date	Opponent	W/L/T	Score	Record
Sept. 4	UNLV[1]	W	1-0	1-0
Sept. 5	Rutgers[1]	L	0-1	1-1
Sept. 10	North Carolina State[2]	W	2-0	2-1
Sept. 11	at Duke[2]	W	2-1	3-1
Sept. 17	at Akron	W	4-0	4-1
Sept. 19	St. Louis	W	3-0	5-1
Sept. 24	at Notre Dame	W	3-0	6-1
Sept. 26	Michigan State	W	2-0	7-1
Oct. 1	Penn State[3]	W	4-1	8-1
Oct. 2	South Carolina[3] (OT)	T	1-1	8-1-1
Oct. 8	UW-Milwaukee	W	6-0	9-1-1
Oct. 10	at Bowling Green	W	5-2	10-1-1
Oct. 15	at Wisconsin	W	5-1	11-1-1
Oct. 16	at Northwestern	W	6-2	12-1-1
Oct. 22	at Illinois State	W	3-1	13-1-1
Oct. 24	Ohio State	W	7-0	14-1-1
Oct. 29	at South Florida[4]	W	3-1	15-1-1
Oct. 31	College of Charleston[4]	W	3-0	16-1-1

Big Ten Tournament (Madison, Wis.)

Date	Opponent	W/L/T	Score	Record
Nov. 6	Penn State	L	0-1	16-2-1

NCAA Tournament

Date	Opponent	W/L/T	Score	Record
Nov. 15	Memphis	W	6-0	17-2-1
Nov. 21	Wisconsin	L	0-1	17-3-1

[1]adidas-MetLife Classic (Bloomington)
[2]Duke Classic (Durham, N.C.)
[3]Notre Dame Classic (South Bend)
[4]South Florida Classic (Tampa, Fla.)

1994   Record: 23-3

Date	Opponent	W/L/T	Score	Record
Sept. 3	South Carolina[1]	W	1-0	1-0
Sept. 4	North Carolina[1]	L	1-2	1-1
Sept. 9	Miami (Ohio)	W	6-0	2-1
Sept. 11	at Kentucky	W	6-1	3-1
Sept. 16	Akron	W	10-0	4-1
Sept. 18	at St. Louis	W	4-0	5-1
Sept. 21	Clemson[2]	W	3-1	6-1
Sept. 23	Notre Dame	W	2-0	7-1
Sept. 25	at Michigan State	W	2-0	8-1
Sept. 30	at Penn State	W	2-1	9-1
Oct. 2	Drake	W	2-0	10-1
Oct. 6	at Butler	W	2-0	11-1
Oct. 9	Bowling Green	W	1-0	12-1
Oct. 14	Wisconsin	W	2-0	13-1
Oct. 16	Northwestern	W	4-0	14-1
Oct. 21	at Evansville	W	3-1	15-1
Oct. 23	at Ohio State	W	1-0	16-1
Oct. 28	Cal State Fullerton[3] (OT)	L	2-3	16-2
Oct. 30	at UCLA[3]	W	2-0	17-2

Big Ten Tournament (Columbus, Ohio)

Date	Opponent	W/L/T	Score	Record
Nov. 11	Wisconsin	W	1-0	18-2
Nov. 13	Penn State	W	3-1	19-2

NCAA Tournament

Date	Opponent	W/L/T	Score	Record
Nov. 20	Notre Dame (OT)	W	1-0	20-2
Nov. 27	Creighton	W	1-0	21-2
Dec. 4	Cal State Fullerton	W	2-1	22-2

NCAA College Cup (Davidson, N.C.)

Date	Opponent	W/L/T	Score	Record
Dec. 9	UCLA	W	4-1	23-2
Dec. 11	Virginia	L	0-1	23-3

[1]adidas-MetLife Classic (Bloomington)
[2]Game of the Week (Davidson, N.C.)
[3]UCLA Classic (Los Angeles)

1995   Record: 14-5-2

Date	Opponent	W/L/T	Score	Record
Sept. 2	North Carolina State[1] (OT)	T	1-1	0-0-1
Sept. 3	Boston University[1]	W	2-0	1-0-1
Sept. 8	at Rutgers (OT)	W	1-0	2-0-1
Sept. 10	Kentucky (OT)	L	0-1	2-1-1
Sept. 15	at Akron	W	1-0	3-1-1
Sept. 17	St. Louis	W	1-0	4-1-1

Date	Opponent	W/L/T	Score	Record
Sept. 22	at Notre Dame (OT)	W	4-2	5-1-1
Sept. 24	Michigan State (OT)	W	1-0	6-1-1
Sept. 29	Penn State	L	1-2	6-2-1
Oct. 1	at Miami (Ohio)	W	3-1	7-2-1
Oct. 6	Butler (OT)	W	1-0	8-2-1
Oct. 8	at Bowling Green	L	1-2	8-3-1
Oct. 13	at Wisconsin	L	0-2	8-4-1
Oct. 15	at Northwestern	W	7-0	9-4-1
Oct. 20	Evansville (OT)	T	2-2	9-4-2
Oct. 22	Ohio State	W	1-0	10-4-2
Oct. 27	UNC-Charlotte[2]	W	2-1	11-4-2
Oct. 29	at Florida International[2]	W	1-0	12-4-2

Big Ten Tournament (East Lansing, Mich.)

Date	Opponent	W/L/T	Score	Record
Nov. 10	Northwestern	W	2-1	13-4-2
Nov. 11	Penn State	W	3-1	14-4-2

NCAA Tournament

Date	Opponent	W/L/T	Score	Record
Nov. 19	Butler	L	0-1	14-5-2

[1]adidas-MetLife Classic (Bloomington)
[2]Florida International Southern Bell Classic (Ft. Lauderdale, Fla.)

1996   Record: 15-3-3

Date	Opponent	W/L/T	Score	Record
Sept. 7	UCLA[1] (OT)	L	0-1	0-1
Sept. 8	Duke[1]	N/A	0-0	0-1
Sept. 14	Marquette[2] (OT)	W	3-2	1-1
Sept. 15	UAB[2] (OT)	T	1-1	1-1-1
Sept. 20	Akron	W	5-0	2-1-1
Sept. 27	Notre Dame	W	3-0	3-1-1
Sept. 29	at Michigan State (OT)	W	2-1	4-1-1
Oct. 4	at Penn State (OT)	T	1-1	4-1-2
Oct. 6	Miami (Ohio)	W	4-0	5-1-2
Oct. 10	at Butler	W	6-1	6-1-2
Oct. 13	Bowling Green	L	0-2	6-2-2
Oct. 18	Wisconsin	W	1-0	7-2-2
Oct. 20	Northwestern	W	11-1	8-2-2
Oct. 24	at Kentucky	W	5-3	9-2-2
Oct. 27	at Ohio State	W	1-0	10-2-2
Nov. 2	at College of Charleston[3]	W	2-1	11-2-2
Nov. 3	South Carolina[3]	W	1-0	12-2-2

Big Ten Tournament (University Park, Pa.)

Date	Opponent	W/L/T	Score	Record
Nov. 16	at Penn State	T	2-2	12-2-3
Nov. 17	Michigan State	W	4-0	13-2-3

NCAA Tournament

Date	Opponent	W/L/T	Score	Record
Nov. 24	Evansville	W	4-1	14-2-3
Dec. 1	Bowling Green	W	2-0	15-2-3
Dec. 8	at Florida International	L	0-1	15-3-3

[1]adidas-MetLife Classic (Bloomington)
[2]IPFW–Three Rivers Classic (Ft. Wayne)
[3]College of Charleston Classic (Charleston, S.C.)

1997   Record: 23-1

Date	Opponent	W/L/T	Score	Record
Sept. 2	at Notre Dame	W	4-0	1-0
Sept. 5	Rutgers[1] (OT)	W	4-3	2-0
Sept. 6	Clemson[1]	W	3-0	3-0
Sept. 12	North Carolina State[2]	W	5-1	4-0
Sept. 13	at Duke[2]	W	2-1	5-0
Sept. 20	Bowling Green[3]	W	1-0	6-0
Sept. 21	Rhode Island[3]	W	6-1	7-0
Sept. 25	Kentucky	W	9-0	8-0
Sept. 28	Michigan State	W	3-0	9-0
Oct. 3	Penn State	W	2-0	10-0
Oct. 5	at Miami (Ohio)	W	4-0	11-0
Oct. 9	Butler	W	6-2	12-0
Oct. 12	Evansville (OT)	W	2-1	13-0
Oct. 17	at Wisconsin	W	4-1	14-0
Oct. 19	at Northwestern	W	4-0	15-0
Oct. 26	Ohio State	W	2-0	16-0
Oct. 31	Stanford[4]	W	2-1	17-0
Nov. 2	at California[4]	W	3-1	18-0

Big Ten Tournament (Bloomington)

Date	Opponent	W/L/T	Score	Record
Nov. 15	Penn State	W	4-0	19-0
Nov. 16	Ohio State	W	1-0	20-0

NCAA Tournament

Date	Opponent	W/L/T	Score	Record
Nov. 23	Butler (3 OT)	W	2-1	21-0
Nov. 30	Bowling Green	W	4-0	22-0
Dec. 7	South Florida	W	6-0	23-0

NCAA College Cup (Richmond, Va.)

Date	Opponent	W/L/T	Score	Record
Dec. 12	UCLA (3 OT)	L	0-1	23-1

[1]adidas-Foot Locker Classic (Bloomington)
[2]Duke adidas Classic (Durham, N.C.)
[3]Butler Classic (Indianapolis)
[4]California Classic (San Francisco)

1998   Record: 23-2

Date	Opponent	W/L/T	Score	Record
Sept. 4	College of Charleston[1]	W	1-0	1-0
Sept. 5	California[1]	W	2-0	2-0
Sept. 11	Florida International[2]	W	6-0	3-0
Sept. 12	at SMU[2]	L	0-2	3-1
Sept. 16	Miami (Ohio)	W	4-0	4-1
Sept. 18	Central Florida[3]	W	3-0	5-1
Sept. 20	Jacksonville[3]	W	4-1	6-1
Sept. 25	Louisville	W	3-0	7-1
Sept. 27	at Michigan State	W	3-0	8-1
Oct. 2	at Penn State (OT)	W	1-0	9-1
Oct. 8	at Butler	W	3-0	10-1
Oct. 11	at Evansville (OT)	W	2-1	11-1
Oct. 16	Wisconsin	W	3-0	12-1
Oct. 18	Northwestern	W	1-0	13-1
Oct. 21	at Kentucky	W	5-0	14-1
Oct. 25	at Ohio State (OT)	W	1-0	15-1
Oct. 30	Loyola Marymount[4]	W	3-0	16-1
Nov. 1	at UCLA[4]	L	1-2	16-2

Big Ten Tournament (Evanston, Ill.)

Date	Opponent	W/L/T	Score	Record
Nov. 14	Wisconsin	W	4-0	17-2
Nov. 15	Penn State (OT)	W	1-0	18-2

NCAA Tournament

Date	Opponent	W/L/T	Score	Record
Nov. 22	Akron (OT)	W	3-2	19-2
Nov. 29	Butler (OT)	W	2-1	20-2
Dec. 6	at Clemson	W	2-1	21-2

NCAA College Cup (Richmond, Va.)

Date	Opponent	W/L/T	Score	Record
Dec. 11	Santa Clara	W	4-0	22-2
Dec. 13	Stanford	W	3-1	23-2

[1]adidas Classic (Bloomington)
[2]SMU Classic (Dallas)
[3]Butler Classic (Indianapolis)
[4]UCLA Soccer Classic (Los Angeles)

1999   Record: 21-3

Date	Opponent	W/L/T	Score	Record
Sept. 3	Maryland[1]	W	1-0	1-0
Sept. 5	St. Louis[1]	L	0-1	1-1
Sept. 11	Yale[2]	L	1-2	1-2
Sept. 12	at Brown[2]	W	5-0	2-2
Sept. 17	Fresno State[3]	W	2-1	3-2
Sept. 19	Texas Christian[3]	W	1-0	4-2
Sept. 23	at Louisville	W	2-0	5-2
Sept. 26	Michigan State	W	2-0	6-2

Date	Opponent	W/L/T	Score	Record
Oct. 1	Penn State	W	4-2	7-2
Oct. 7	Butler	W	5-0	8-2
Oct. 10	Evansville	W	6-0	9-2
Oct. 15	at Wisconsin	W	2-0	10-2
Oct. 17	at Northwestern	W	1-0	11-2
Oct. 20	Kentucky	W	4-2	12-2
Oct. 24	Ohio State	W	2-1	13-2
Oct. 29	at Florida International[4] (OT)	W	1-0	14-2
Oct. 31	James Madison[4]	L	0-2	14-3

Big Ten Tournament (East Lansing, Mich.)

Date	Opponent	W/L/T	Score	Record
Nov. 13	Northwestern	W	2-0	15-3
Nov. 14	Penn State (2OT)	W	2-1	16-3

NCAA Tournament

Date	Opponent	W/L/T	Score	Record
Nov. 21	Kentucky (OT)	W	1-0	17-3
Nov. 28	Washington	W	2-0	18-3
Dec. 5	Penn State	W	3-0	19-3

NCAA College Cup (Charlotte, N.C.)

Date	Opponent	W/L/T	Score	Record
Dec. 11	UCLA (4OT)	W	3-2	20-3
Dec. 12	Santa Clara	W	1-0	21-3

[1]adidas Classic (Bloomington)
[2]Brown/adidas Classic (Providence, R.I.)
[3]Nike/Snickers Soccerfest IV (Indianapolis)
[4]FIU Bell South Classic (Miami, Fla.)

2000   Record: 16-7

Date	Opponent	W/L/T	Score	Record
Sept. 1	Portland[1]	L	0-3	0-1
Sept. 2	UCLA[1]	L	1-2	0-2
Sept. 8	at Maryland[2] (OT)	W	2-1	1-2
Sept. 10	Virginia[2]	W	2-1	2-2
Sept. 13	IUPUI	W	2-0	3-2
Sept. 15	Creighton[3]	L	1-4	3-3
Sept. 17	Florida International[3]	W	1-0	4-3
Sept. 21	Louisville	W	2-0	5-3
Sept. 24	at Michigan State	W	1-0	6-3
Sept. 30	at Penn State	W	3-2	7-3
Oct. 6	at Butler	W	1-0	8-3
Oct. 8	Michigan	W	7-0	9-3
Oct. 13	Wisconsin	W	3-1	10-3
Oct. 15	Northwestern	W	4-1	11-3
Oct. 18	at Kentucky	W	2-0	12-3
Oct. 22	at Ohio State	W	1-0	13-3
Nov. 4	Stanford[4] (OT)	L	0-1	13-4
Nov. 5	Cal-Berkeley[4]	L	1-2	13-5

Big Ten Tournament (Columbus)

Date	Opponent	W/L/T	Score	Record
Nov. 13	at Ohio State	L	0-1	13-6

NCAA Tournament

Date	Opponent	W/L/T	Score	Record
Nov. 18	San Jose State	W	4-0	14-6
Nov. 25	at Washington	W	2-1	15-6
Dec. 2	at UNC	W	1-0	16-6

NCAA College Cup (Charlotte, N.C.)

Date	Opponent	W/L/T	Score	Record
Dec. 8	Creighton (3OT)	L	2-1	16-7

[1]adidas Classic (Bloomington)
[2]Maryland Soccer Classic
[3]Butler Classic (Indianapolis)
[4]Cal-Berkeley Soccer Classic (Berkeley)

2001   Record: 18-4-1

Date	Opponent	W/L/T	Score	Record
Aug. 31	St. John's[1]	L	1-2	0-1
Sept. 1	Kentucky[1] (2OT)	W	1-0	1-1
Sept. 8	Washington[2]	W	1-0	2-1
Sept. 9	at Portland[2]	L	0-1	2-2
Sept. 20	at Louisville	W	4-0	3-2
Sept. 23	Michigan State	W	3-0	4-2
Sept. 28	Penn State	W	3-1	5-2
Oct. 4	Butler	W	3-0	6-2
Oct. 7	at Michigan	W	3-0	7-2
Oct. 12	at Wisconsin	W	4-0	8-2
Oct. 14	at Northwestern	W	3-0	9-2
Oct. 17	Notre Dame	L	0-1	9-3
Oct. 20	Ohio State	W	1-0	10-3
Oct. 26	at Rutgers	W	1-0	11-3
Oct. 28	at Princeton	T	1-1	11-3-1
Nov. 4	IUPUI	W	6-0	12-3-1

Big Ten Tournament (Madison, Wis.)

Date	Opponent	W/L/T	Score	Record
Nov. 9	Michigan (3OT)	W	1-0	13-3-1
Nov. 11	Michigan State	W	2-0	14-3-1

NCAA Tournament

Date	Opponent	W/L/T	Score	Record
Nov. 25	Michigan State	W	1-0	15-3-1
Dec. 2	Rutgers	W	3-0	16-3-1
Dec. 9	Clemson	W	2-0	17-3-1

NCAA College Cup (Columbus, Ohio)

Date	Opponent	W/L/T	Score	Record
Dec. 14	St. John's (2OT)	W	2-1	18-3-1
Dec. 16	North Carolina	L	0-2	18-4-1

[1]adidas/IU Credit Union Classic
[2]Portland Classic

2002   Record: 15-4-2

Date	Opponent	W/L/T	Score	Record
Aug. 30	Rutgers[1] (2OT)	T	0-0	0-0-1
Aug. 31	Clemson[1] (2OT)	T	1-1	0-0-2
Sept. 6	William & Mary[2]	W	2-1	1-0-2
Sept. 7	at St. John's[2]	L	0-3	1-1-2
Sept. 10	Louisville	W	2-0	2-1-2
Sept. 13	Air Force[3]	W	2-0	3-1-2
Sept. 15	Hartwick[3]	W	1-0	4-1-2
Sept. 22	at Michigan State	W	6-1	5-1-2
Sept. 27	at Penn State (2OT)	W	1-0	6-1-2
Oct. 3	at Butler	W	2-0	7-1-2
Oct. 6	Michigan (2OT)	W	2-1	8-1-2
Oct. 11	Wisconsin	W	5-1	9-1-2
Oct. 13	Northwestern	W	1-0	10-1-2
Oct. 16	at Kentucky	W	2-1	11-1-2
Oct. 20	at Ohio State	W	4-2	12-1-2
Oct. 25	at Cal State Fullerton	L	1-0	12-2-2
Oct. 27	UC-Santa Barbara[4]	W	3-1	13-2-2
Nov. 3	IUPUI (OT)	W	2-1	14-2-2

Big Ten Tournament (State College, Pa.)

Nov. 15	at Penn State (OT; PKs)	L	2-1	14-3-2

NCAA Tournament

Nov. 27	Notre Dame	W	1-0	15-3-2
Dec. 1	at UCONN	L	1-0	15-4-2

[1]adidas/IU Credit Union Classic

[2]St. John's Classic (Kingsport, N.Y.)

[3]Butler SoccerFest (Indianapolis)

[4]played in Fullerton, Calif.

2003   Record: 17-3-5

Aug. 29	California[1]	W	3-0	1-0
Aug. 30	UAB[1] (2OT)	T	0-0	1-0-1
Sept. 5	Georgetown[2] (2OT)	T	2-2	1-0-2
Sept. 6	UCONN[2]	L	1-2	1-1-2
Sept. 12	Akron[3] (OT)	L	0-1	1-2-2
Sept. 14	Fresno State[3]	W	3-1	2-2-2
Sept. 18	at Notre Dame (2OT)	L	0-1	2-3-2
Sept. 21	Michigan State (2OT)	T	1-1	2-3-3
Oct. 2	Butler (2OT)	T	1-1	2-3-4
Oct. 5	at Michigan (OT)	W	2-1	3-3-4
Oct. 10	at Wisconsin	W	3-0	4-3-4
Oct. 12	at Northwestern	W	3-0	5-3-4
Oct. 15	IUPUI	W	1-0	6-3-4
Oct. 19	Ohio State	W	3-0	7-3-4

Date	Opponent	W/L/T	Score	Record
Oct. 24	St. Louis	W	2-1	8-3-4
Oct. 29	at Louisville	W	2-0	9-3-4
Nov. 2	Kentucky	W	1-0	10-3-4
Nov. 8	Penn State	W	3-2	11-3-4

Big Ten Championships (Bloomington)

Nov. 14	Wisconsin	W	1-0	12-3-4
Nov. 16	Penn State (OT; PKs)	T	1-1	12-3-5

NCAA Tournament

Nov. 26	Kentucky (2OT)	W	2-1	13-3-5
Nov. 30	Virginia Commonwealth	W	5-0	14-3-5
Dec. 6	at UCLA	W	2-1	15-3-5

NCAA College Cup (Columbus, Ohio)

Dec. 12	Santa Clara (2OT)	W	1-0	16-3-5
Dec. 14	St. John's	W	2-1	17-3-5

[1]adidas/IU Credit Union Classic (Bloomington)

[2]University of Connecticut Classic (Storrs, Conn.)

[3]Notre Dame Berticelli Memorial Tournament (South Bend)

Note: Photographs are indicated with **boldface** type.

KATHRYN L. KNAPP *is a freelance journalist. She has covered Indiana University men's soccer since 1995 and the Chicago Fire of Major League Soccer since 1999. Knapp graduated from Indiana University in 1999 with a B.A. in journalism. She lives in Hammond, Indiana.*

Sponsoring Editor: Janet Rabinowitch
Copy Editor: Jane Lyle
Book and Cover Designer: Pamela Rude
Compositor: Tony Brewer